PRAISE FOR *DEATH BLOSSOMS*

"Uncompromising, disturbing . . . Abu-Ja▌
of a man whose impending death embo▌
without fear of consequence."

"Abu-Jamal's words flow like the sap fi▌
capturing the essence of life."

—*Library Journal*

"Vigorous social critiques and moving essays on matters of faith . . . the flame
of Abu-Jamal's keen intellect and irrepressible soul burns brightly, illuminating
each mind that opens to his wise words."

—*ALA Booklist*

"A brilliant, lucid meditation on the moral obligation of political commitment
by a deeply ethical—and deeply wronged—human being. Mumia should be
freed, now."

—Henry Louis Gates Jr.

"A brilliant, powerful book by a prophetic writer. Mumia refuses to allow his
spirit to be broken by the forces of injustice; his language glows with an af-
firming flame."

—Jonathan Kozol

"Crucial reading for all opponents of the death penalty—and for those who
support it, too."

—Katha Pollitt, *The Nation*

"If Mumia Abu-Jamal has nothing important to say, why are so many powerful
people trying to kill him and shut him up? Read him."

—John Edgar Wideman

"For years in my classrooms I have watched *Death Blossoms* do its luminous
work. It has awakened the conscience of so many of my student readers.
Once awakened they begin to shoulder the disciplines of a revolutionary
knowing, its moral passion, historical precision and clarity of reason. No
wonder repressive powers seek death for this prisoner of conscience. Alas
for them, Mumia still lives. From streets to classrooms and back, *Death
Blossoms* keeps opening up conscience, heart and mind for our revolutionary work."

—Mark Lewis Taylor, Professor of Theology and Culture at Princeton
Theological Seminary, and author of *The Theological and the Political:
On the Weight of the World*

"Mumia Abu-Jamal has challenged us to see the prison at the center of a long history of U.S. oppression, and he has inspired us to keep faith with ordinary struggles against injustice under the most terrible odds and circumstances. Written more than two decades ago, *Death Blossoms* helps us to see beyond prison walls; it is as timely and as necessary as the day it was published."

—Nikhil Pal Singh, author of *Race and America's Long War*

"Targeted by the FBI's COINTELPRO for his revolutionary politics, imprisoned, and sentenced to death, Mumia found freedom in resistance. His reflections here—on race, spirituality, struggle, and life—illuminate this path to freedom for us all."

—Joshua Bloom, co-author with Waldo E. Martin Jr. of *Black Against Empire: The History and Politics of the Black Panther Party*

"In this revised edition of his groundbreaking work, *Death Blossoms*, convicted death row prisoner Mumia Abu-Jamal tackles hard and existential questions, searching for God and a greater meaning in a caged life that may be cut short if the state has its way and takes his life. As readers follow Mumia's journey through his poems, short essays, and longer musings, they will learn not only about this singular individual who has retained his humanity despite the ever present threat of execution, but also about themselves and our society: what we are willing to tolerate and who we are willing to cast aside. If there is any justice, Mumia will prevail in his battle for his life and for his freedom."

—Lara Bazelon, author of *Rectify: The Power of Restorative Justice After Wrongful Conviction*

"For over three decades, the words of Mumia Abu-Jamal have been tools many young activists have used to connect the dots of empire, racism and resistance. The welcome reissue of *Death Blossoms* is a chance to reconnect with Abu-Jamal's prophetic voice, one that needs to be heard now more than ever."

—Hilary Moore and James Tracy, co-authors of *No Fascist USA!, The John Brown Anti-Klan Committee and Lessons for Today*

DEATH BLOSSOMS

MUMIA
A B U - J A M A L

DEATH BLOSSOMS

REFLECTIONS FROM A PRISONER OF CONSCIENCE
Expanded Edition

FOREWORD BY
CORNEL WEST

PREFACE BY
JULIA WRIGHT

CITY LIGHTS BOOKS | OPEN MEDIA SERIES
SAN FRANCISCO

Open Media Series Editor: Greg Ruggiero.

Cover art by Intifada Street, "Mumia Will Prevail, Mumia Will be Free," 2019.

Frontispiece photograph by Jennifer Beach.

The passages by Kahlil Gibran on pages 8 and 101 are excerpted from his book *The Prophet*. Copyright 1923 by Kahlil Gibran and renewed 1951 by Administrators C.T.A. of Kahlil Gibran Estate and Mary G. Gibran. Reprinted by permission of Alfred A. Knopf, Inc.

Library of Congress Cataloging-in-Publication Data

Names: Abu-Jamal, Mumia, author. | West, Cornel, writer of foreword. | Wright, Julia, 1942- writer of preface.
Title: Death blossoms : reflections from a prisoner of conscience / Mumia Abu-Jamal ; foreword by Cornel West ; preface by Julia Wright.
Description: Expanded edition. | San Francisco : City Lights Books, [2020] | Series: Open media series | Includes bibliographical references. | Summary: "Profound meditations on life, death, freedom, family, and faith, written by radical Black journalist, Mumia Abu-Jamal, while he was awaiting his execution"— Provided by publisher.
Identifiers: LCCN 2019026920 (print) | LCCN 2019026921 (ebook) | ISBN 9780872867970 (paperback) | ISBN 9780872868014 (ebook)
Subjects: LCSH: Abu-Jamal, Mumia. | Death row inmates—United States—Biography. | African American prisoners—Biography. | Prisoners' writings, American.
Classification: LCC HV8699.U5 A33 2020 (print) | LCC HV8699.U5 (ebook) | DDC 364.66092 [B]—dc23
LC record available at https://lccn.loc.gov/2019026920
LC ebook record available at https://lccn.loc.gov/2019026921

City Lights Books are published at the City Lights Bookstore
261 Columbus Avenue, San Francisco, CA 94133
www.citylights.com

CONTENTS

TO THOSE

nameless ones who came before

and are no more,

to those who leapt

to dark, salty depths,

to those who battled

against all odds,

to those who would give birth

to gods,

to those who would not yield—

To those who came before,

to those who are to come,

I dedicate this shield.

M.A.J.

PREFACE TO THE 2020 EDITION

Mumia Abu-Jamal

Imagine knowing that you will soon die.

Imagine not only knowing the exact date your life will end, but that you will die an unnatural death.

Imagine knowing that you will be deliberately killed by the authorities of the state in which you live.

Imagine, if you can, that you were shot by police, arrested, tortured, jailed, and sentenced to be executed as a result of court proceedings that Amnesty International declared were "in violation of minimum international standards that govern fair trial procedures and the use of the death penalty."

Imagine spending your last days alone inside a small prison cell in a hellish place called death row.

What would you *think* about as the clock ticked down on you?

What would you *dream*?

What would you *hope?*

How would you make sense of the things you heard, saw, and felt as the date of your execution neared?

To read this book, one of my first literary endeavors, a generation after its tumultuous birth, is to experience the smells of fear, trepidation, and the genuine threat of execution that I lived with as a forced inhabitant of Pennsylvania's death row.

But against the canvas of unfreedom, death, and barbarity portrayed in the pages ahead, aspects of our humanity blossom into relief. Such is the intention of this book. For *Death Blossoms* is, above all, a meditation on the faith of the oppressed.

Such faith may take many forms, but all are shaped and informed by resilience against oppression. It thus utilizes the voices, dreams, and poetics of the oppressed to imagine freedom. To understand that faith, we swim to the lowest depths of society and find, to our surprise, the beating of a multitude of hearts—the *cris de cœur*—of those sentenced to the nothingness of death row in all its awfulness and all its awesomeness.

Who can forget the voices of those so consigned—people who sit for decades awaiting the state's siren song to call them to surrender their last breath to the Grim Reaper? It is a forbidding task. A work of

venturing to that City of Sighs that should, with
a certain cruel justification, bear a legend etched
into stone worthy of the inscription in the arch over
Dante's Gate of Hell: "*Lasciate ogne speranza, voi
ch'intrate*"—"Abandon all hope, ye who enter here."

It has been many long years and almost ten books
since I lived in the crisp white pages of *Death Blossoms*. Around that time, I had come within thirteen
days of an execution date, and would soon be given
another exact date to die. I handwrote the pages of
this book on three-ring-binder paper after meeting
members of a remarkable group called the Bruderhof, a community located in the highlands of western
Pennsylvania dedicated to the vision that "another life
is possible"—a "love your neighbor, share everything"
life "where there are no rich or poor. Where everyone is cared for, everyone belongs, and everyone
can contribute." The Bruderhof were, as refugees
from Hitler's Germany, anti-fascist, anti-racist, and
deeply opposed to the death penalty. I found them
intriguing. We conversed together about their ideas,
and out of those conversations—and the sense that
I might soon be killed by the state—grew *Death
Blossoms*.

Much has changed since that moment in time; but
woefully, much has also remained the same. As of

January 2019, 2,664 souls still languish on death row in the United States, 145 of them in Pennsylvania.

Over the years, some who were sentenced to die have made the leap across the moat into *real* life: Freedom. Most of those have done well, but all have nightmares of their years on death row: its cacophony, its rank smells, its bits of sheer madness, its ever-present threat of violence.

As I write these words, a lawsuit is making its way through the tunnels of the Pennsylvania judiciary seeking the abolition of the House of Death. But as it is now, more than 140 souls still languish in the twilight of death row. One man—Sug—was forced to wait eleven years—*eleven years!*—for a retrial. When it finally took place, the district attorney continued to argue for Sug's execution, but a Philadelphia jury refused to send him back to the Row.

Thus, the stories that originally populated the pages of *Death Blossoms* continue to bloom in dark, dank places. Souls weep, souls spin, souls creep fitfully toward the light. Souls sing, souls keen, and souls soar toward their highest and best selves, despite the obscenity of death row and its political architects.

Death row may have shrunken in size, but it hasn't lost its social and political significance. Politicians continue to play the Game of Fear that allows them to construct more ways to exercise state terror against the wretched of the earth.

But a new wind may be blowing through the air; the cries of groups like Black Lives Matter and its spirited affiliates nationwide have burst open doors once chained and cemented closed.

Young people, bold as life, have identified these sites of state terror and are calling for their abolition. They have already run repressive district attorneys out of office in a half dozen cities across America.

May this work, now reaching its third life, give fuel and heft to their noble efforts, for only social movements truly change history.

From Life Row,

Mumia Abu-Jamal
Autumn 2019

FOREWORD

Cornel West

The passionate and prophetic voice of
Mumia Abu-Jamal challenges us to wrestle with
the most distinctive feature of present-day America: the relative erosion of the systems of caring
and nurturing. This frightening reality, which
renders more and more people unloved and un-
wanted, results primarily from several fundamental processes. There are, for example, the forces
of our unregulated capitalist market, which have
yielded not only immoral levels of wealth inequal-
ity and economic insecurity but also personal isolation and psychic disorientation. Then there is the
legacy of white supremacy, which—in subtle and
not-so-subtle ways—continues to produce new
forms of geographical segregation, job ceilings,
and social tension. We can also see how, in other
arenas, oppressive ideologies and persisting bigot-
ries (like patriarchy and homophobia) smother the
possibility of healthy and humane relations among
men and women. In short, our capitalist "civiliza-
tion" is killing our minds, bodies, and souls in the
name of the American Dream.

As one who has lived on the night-side of
this dream—unjustly imprisoned for a crime he
did not commit—Mumia Abu-Jamal speaks to us
of the institutional injustice and spiritual impover-
ishment that permeates our culture. He reminds
us of things most fellow citizens would rather
deny, ignore, or evade. And, like the most powerful critics of our society—from Herman Melville,
Theodore Dreiser, and Nathaniel West to Ann
Petry, Richard Wright, Toni Morrison, and Eugene
O'Neill—he forces us to grapple with the most
fundamental question facing this country: What
does it profit a nation to conquer the whole world
and lose its soul? After decades of nightmarish jail
conditions, Mumia Abu-Jamal's soul is not only in-
tact but still flourishing—just as the nation's soul
withers. Will we ever listen to and learn from our
bloodstained prophets?

Cambridge, Mass

PREFACE

Julia Wright

> Under a government that imprisons any man un-
> justly, the true place for a just man is also a prison.
>
> *Henry David Thoreau, 1817–1862*

> Does the silk-worm expend her yellow labours for
> thee? For thee does she undo herself?
>
> *Cyril Tourneur, c. 1575–1626*

There are all sorts of silences—as many perhaps as there are textures to our sense of touch or shades of color to the eye. But I will always remember the extraordinary silence that fell over a Pittsburgh courtroom on October 13, 1995, when an African-American journalist and world-known author walked in slow motion, his feet in chains, to present testimony in his own civil suit against his prison (SCI Greene) and Pennsylvania's Department of Corrections for violation of his human rights. His name—Mumia Abu-Jamal.

Ripples of silence froze in his shackled footsteps. As if on'a move waves could be stilled, this was a silence of total paradox: the volatile, scarcely hidden presence of loaded police weapons targeting

the reined-in love of members of the family in the
courtroom—men, women, and children who have
been unable to touch him for fourteen years. I was
reminded of Coleridge's uncannily arrested sea: a
spell cast against the forces of life. Having at last
reached the stand in hi-tech noiselessness (America now produces *silent* chains for her prisoners'
feet), a gentle giant spoke and was unbound by his
own words.

The defense team for SCI Greene proceeded to
interrogate Mumia, asking him repeatedly whether
he knew he was violating prison rules when he
wrote his book *Live From Death Row.* "Yes," quietly. (A tremor through the silence.) Did he know
he was violating the same rules when he accepted
payment for articles, commentaries, etc. . . ? "Yes,"
in soft-spoken, vibrant tones. (The silence stirs.)
Did he know that the current punishment for entering into "the illicit business of writing" behind bars
was ninety days in the "hole" and a prison investigation justifying the monitoring of his mail and
limited access to all categories of visitors including
family, paralegals, spiritual counselors, the press?
"Yes," patiently, wearily. (The silence vibrates but
congeals again, oily and ominous.)

"Why then, if you knew, did you go ahead and write
that book?"

"Because, whatever the cost to me, I knew I *had* to offer to the world a window into the souls of those who, like me, suffer barbaric conditions on America's death rows. . . ."

American silence shattered like cheap glass. Judge Benson suspended the hearing. . . .

THE BOOK YOU ARE about to read, Mumia's second "crime" since *Live From Death Row*, breaks through American silence yet again as its author shares with us his prison-brewed antidotes against bars of silence more deadly than the cold steel he touches every day.

In the recent HBO-Channel 4-Otmoor documentary *Mumia Abu-Jamal: A Case for Reasonable Doubt?*, Mumia finds words to tell us about the inhuman experience of sensory isolation he has been exposed to for two-thirds of a generation:

Once someone closes that door, there is no sound. There is the sound of silence in your cell. There is the sound of an air-conditioner and the sound of silence, the sound you create in your own cell. The sense of isolation is all but total, because you're cut off even from the sonic presence of people. Imagine going into your bathroom, locking the door behind you, and not leaving that bathroom, except

for an hour or two [each day] . . . and staying
in that bathroom for the rest of your natural
life, with a date to die.

In *Death Blossoms,* Mumia's victories against such
sensory deprivation are as many prizes he has
wrested from prison. ("Prize" and "prison" share the
same root meaning: "to seize.") However, he does
not present us with ready-made, do-it-yourself,
take-away prescriptions: that would be too simple.
If a pattern of anti-carceral antidotes is to be found
in the pages that follow, it is for us to learn how
to detect them, just as Henry James believed that
readers need to reach a certain stage of lucidity
before they can make out the hidden "figure" in a
writer's "carpet."

Nothing, Mumia lets us know, can begin without the *word.* Writing behind locked doors gives
durable sound to prison silence, spiritual distance
from a madding crowd of politicians and elected
judges whose careers are built on the blood of
others, creative dimension to the sound and fury of
a world lost. In writing, there is a renewed bonding: unshackled hands grasping notebook, fingers
touching pencil, pencil touching paper, paper
touched by readers who are in turn touched by
meaning. And *something* is badly needed to prevent the outside world from receding, to arrest the
slowing-down of the metabolism of exchange with

one's remembered community. Do colors pale and falter with Plexiglas filtering? Is there a sepia-like transmutation due to the overexposure of much revisited memories?

Death Blossoms seems bathed in a shimmering translucency, as if remembered color 'n' sound are bleeding out of prison-reality, and this existential hemorrhage can be stopped only by the "brilliant etching of writing upon the brain."

CAN ALL THE CENTURIES of world philosophy even begin to visualize the dreams and nightmares of our death row inmates? The raw stuff of dreams draws on the immediacy of the sentient world—but when that world is suppressed, what happens to those dreaming processes which constitute one of the foundations of human sanity? Rollo May has written about that existential pain at the heart of all human exile: the inability to go home. Homelessness, like noiselessness and lack of physical contact, is at the core of American "correction." It is the experience of being at home or not, of being able to go home or not, that sustains the sense of self or begins to shatter it. And it is one of the amazing strengths of this book that Mumia has turned his mind into his home, showing us in the process how out-of-our-minds we may have become in the "open" society outside. Mumia's inner home is so limitless that when we exit this book, it is into our own materialistic, petty reality-cells that we enter, apparently of our own "free" will.

This is not classic autobiography or even "intellectual" biography. It is the narrative of an escape from prison into the liberated territory of the mind, a pacing not of the cage but of the psyche, a jogging not in the pen but in the open space Mumia calls "reaching beyond." We are privileged that he takes us with him on a liberating tour of his own freedom. Resolutely on'a move within his own spiritual quest, Mumia makes us understand that "free" men and women can imprison and arrest their own revolutions just as "inmates" can set free a boundless revolution of the mind. As Frantz Fanon, the late psychiatrist and freedom fighter, wrote in his *Wretched of the Earth,* "Imperialism leaves behind germs of rot which we must clinically detect and remove from our land but from our minds as well."

Our minds are indeed bombarded with media hype and racial stereotypes. Who does not recall the Disneyland face of a womanchild tearfully describing (for primetime consumption) the black "monster" who murdered her two small boys? Except that this killer turned out to be the figment of her own homicidal imagination. . . . Yet how many Mumia Abu-Jamals were arrested or harassed before the truth was duly established? Who does not remem-

ber a Boston-based Italian-American as he testified, convincingly, to witnessing the murder of his
wife by a black "thug?" Except that this dark fiend
turned out to be a projection straight out of the
husband's criminal mind. . . . But, meanwhile, how
many Abu-Jamals? Who can forget a tear-streaked
widow telling over and over again how the defendant (Mumia) smiled diabolically as the prosecution showed the jury the blood-stained shirt of her
policeman-husband? Except that the minutes of the
trial prove that Judge Sabo had barred Mumia from
the courtroom that day. . . . And so the pattern
repeats itself as we are told that a certain Wesley Cook, a.k.a. Mumia Abu-Jamal, killed a police
officer who happened to be brutalizing his brother. But who is the real Mumia beyond these false,
cold-blooded projections?

Death Blossoms is a personal *and* collective answer
to this question, a generous and human song of
innocence for all the unseen, voiceless men and
women imprisoned by guilty stereotypes way before they set foot in a penitentiary.

Predictably, another "invisible man" haunts this
case: he was seen running away from the scene
of the shooting by at least three witnesses (Dessie
Hightower, William Singletary, Veronica Jones), and
all have since spoken up concerning the police in-
timidation they underwent simply for insisting that

this man was not a figment of their black folks'
imagination. . . .

ALTHOUGH MUMIA'S LIFE–FORCES are sealed off
and preyed upon by a carceral onslaught tanta-
mount to hi-tech slavery, he distills in these pages
the ultimate rebuttal of his imprisonment: mental
and spiritual autarchy.

Death Blossoms displays a deceptively simple
meshing of form and content. In fact, one of the
most fascinating figures in Mumia's "carpet" is
quite literally the carpet itself, the weaving of a
web of words. Revealingly, towards the end of the
book, Norman, an inmate, marvels at a spider's
defiance of prison rules as it spins its web under
his sink. Mumia, who soon discovers a spider of
his own, weaves anecdote into antidote, and we
begin to see that the book we hold in our hands
is also a web spun out of the creative threads of
a mind-made home; just as Anansi, the spider of
ancient African folklore, is the source of a life-web
unraveled from within.

As is uncannily the case with much of Mumia's
writing, the psychological truth is also borne out
scientifically. Randy Lewis, a molecular biologist
who has been studying spiders' secrets for years,
has recently written that "spider silk absorbs more

energy before it breaks than any other material on earth." The writing in *Death Blossoms* is as prison-proof as the silk for vests, currently derived from imprisoned, anesthetized spiders, is bullet proof. And from his carceral lab, Mumia's word-threads reach through and beyond prison bars; they are symbols of the essential twine of bonding with those on the outside. Together they form a web which is an almost literal image for those "holes in the soul" he writes of. But the same web also healingly re-creates in prison the reality of "the whole connected web of nature" and holds us all together as a community in spite of the most brutal assaults. As he notes in reference to the bonds that unite his beloved brothers and sisters of MOVE even after numerous sinister, programmed attempts to destroy their community: "Using neither nails nor lumber, John Africa constructed from the fabric of the heart a tightly cohesive body."

Many of us will not emerge from this book unsnared, for to the extent that we cannot deny the knowledge of what we have read, we are faced with a vital question: Knowing what we know, having become witnesses, can we continue to live and let die?

DEATH BLOSSOMS raises the issue of the innocence of one man—any man—at the hands of an elitist society that manufactures and projects its guilt upon its citizens in order to enrich itself. I am reminded here of my father's character, Fred Daniels, in *The Man Who Lived Underground*. Pursued by the police for a crime he did not commit, Daniels is robbed of his innocence and escapes underground into the city's sewers to avoid capture. As he tries to survive in hiding by resorting to stealing, he takes to peering through cellar doors and invisibly watches others being robbed of *their* innocence as they are punished for *his* thefts. After an old watchman falsely accused on his account commits suicide, Daniels understands from the depths of his netherworld that we are *all* robbed of our innocence and are therefore *all* condemned to guilt. He emerges from the sewers with the urge to share this truth with the world:

> If he could show them what he had seen,
> then they would feel what he had felt, and
> they in turn would show it to others, and
> those others would feel as they had felt, and
> soon everybody would be governed by the
> same impulse of pity.

Similar threads of poignant hope and faith in justice run through *Death Blossoms*, making visible witnesses of us all. Veronica Jones, a hounded witness in Mumia's case, was moved by the same impulse when she recently came forward to set a false record straight, but she was arrested at the stand for sticking to the truth of what she saw—a man running away—and for courageously accepting the responsibility that goes with taking the truth out of the "underground."

Our America, geographically so vast and rich, historically so young and green, has traditionally preferred the materialism of *space* to the invisible threads *time* spins through her landscapes and the experience of her restless peoples. Mumia's writing reconnects us with a much-needed sense of continuity, with the history of our birth as a people on western shores through the Middle Passage, with our ensuing struggle down through time, ongoing, on'a move.

For Mumia, a wholistic struggle—the warp and woof of it—unfolds not only in terms of space-oriented internationalism, but also through the transgenerational glue contained in the web parabole. It is sadly ironical, though, that such an appreciation of the spiritual essence of time should come from a death row inmate who lacks the material wealth that buys life-time in America. But Mumia, with characteristic selflessness, enjoins us to look beyond ourselves at the fragile blooms of our children, and help them "dwell in the house of tomorrow," where we may not be.

A BLOSSOM IS one of the life forms most bound up with the message of time. The fruit it becomes holds in its flesh the memory of the grand bud that came before it, and the foretaste of its passage through rot. According to the most haunting of blues, sung by the sister with the eternal magnolia in her hair, there were many "strange fruit" hanging from our Southern trees. But do our landscapes remember? According to legend, death flowers (also called "mandragore") grew under innocent men who had swung high. These blooms held wondrous powers of fertility and continuum in the hands of the damned of the earth.

As I was reading the manuscript of *Death Blossoms,* I received a deeply moving letter from Mumia recounting his grief at the violent death of Tupac Shakur—a Panther family child, a promising but unfulfilled cub nipped in the bud. "What loss!" Mumia writes. "The son of a Panther who never knew his mother's glory; who called himself a 'thug;' who never realized his truest self, his truest power." Mumia's words will strike a deep chord in those of us who have had to teach our children to become mental guerrillas, and to thread their way through the grim statistics of their own mortality. "Every two hours, one of you dies of gunshot wounds," we force ourselves to teach them.

MUMIA'S INABILITY to touch the grandchildren born to him while on death row is, microcosmically, a double bind experienced by far too many in our decaying "communities:" the intergenerational connections of life are eroded, foreshortened at both ends of our life spans. Targeted by the FBI as a child, Mumia cannot bond with his own children, or theirs—and all have been robbed. My father, Richard Wright, would have met my children and theirs, had he not died in his prime, in unelucidated circumstances. Our generations are torn asunder and brushed aside like cobwebs; they are cut off and isolated—as if on their own death row.

Over half a century after *Native Son*, Bigger—my paper brother—still haunts America, because in his premature death at the hands of the state, there was a foretaste of coming rot. Tupac? Another real-life native son in the long chain since decimation. We live and breathe this state of recurrent loss! We need to be able to find the right rites to mourn so many thousands gone, if only to prevent the next ones from going. Because those slain in childhood will have no children. . . .

It is a healing strength of this book that Mumia, who lives at such mortal risk, can hand us the connective strands of a net to throw far over the great divide, towards generations of children we may never get to know or see or touch. But as he makes clear, we can love them ahead, preventively. And maybe this bond-net, flung far across time as a Love Supreme, will keep them from going too unfortified, too gentle into the bad night of renewed bondage.

Baudelaire's *Les Fleurs du Mal* and Wilde's *Ballad of Reading Gaol* are prime examples of forbidden works written and banned at the end of the nineteenth century, only to become universally loved in the twentieth.

And so here are Mumia Abu-Jamal's *Death Blossoms* — timelessly.

Paris
October 1996

TO THE READER

Steve Wiser

The corridors leading to death row at SCI Greene, Pennsylvania's state-of-the-art supermax, are spanking new. Floor tiles gleam like glass; off-white block walls blend with steel blue window frames and hand rails; smells of wax and lemon-scented detergents permeate the hallways. Even the germs are killed. It's like a hospital—except for one thing: the absence of humanity.

Electronic devices control and monitor every human motion. Cleverly concealed video cameras beam silently from every angle; small speakers crackle in concrete walls. From behind thick glass panels, uniformed guards follow each step. It is enough to make one feel naked, for—literally—the very walls have eyes and ears.

At the end of the long, empty passage is a set of double, remotely controlled doors; beyond them a bleak guard station serves as the command center of L-5. It is the epicenter of this industrial edifice. Yet here one comes face to face with what the system tries hardest to conceal: humanity. Humanity, in all its warmth, richness, and earthiness.

I first met Mumia Abu-Jamal in May, 1995. I had no idea what to expect. I had visited numerous prisons before, from Bastille-like fortresses in Great Britain to Nigerian hell-holes where (instead of razor wire) the walls were lined with vultures, their hideous shriveled heads peering this way and that. But I had never been to a death house.

DEATH ROW WAS A SHOCK. But I was even less prepared to meet the man I had come to visit there: a tall, athletically built African-American whose *joie de vivre* filled his tiny visiting compartment and seemed to overflow, through the Plexiglas partition separating us, into mine. Sitting there opposite him, I discovered a brilliant, compassionate, hearty, articulate man—a man of rare character, tempered and profoundly deepened by suffering.

From the outset, Mumia and I found ourselves communicating heart to heart. To a passing guard, it must have been a strange sight: two cellmates, as it were—one a bald, white minister from a religious order, the other an African-American inmate whose long dreadlocks and urban savvy betrayed an entirely different background.

Even more strange was our discovery of the common values and viewpoints shared by our spiritual families—Mumia's beloved brothers and sisters in the MOVE Organization, and my fellow members of the Bruderhof, a community movement grounded in New Testament teachings. The more we learned about each other, the closer we felt.

As my weekly visits to Mumia continued, all of us at the Bruderhof became increasingly aware of the blatant injustices of his trial—and increasingly active in the international campaign to protest his death sentence. We joined rallies, wrote to government officials and newspaper editors, and printed his writings in our journal, *The Plough*. Not surprisingly, we were met with plenty of criticism, and many who had previously claimed to be our friends censured us for "meddling" in such radical "politics." On the other hand, we gained hundreds of new friends, including death row inmates, writers, artists, and rappers, social workers, teachers, activists, and other religious and secular groups who stand in opposition to the death penalty. We have been deeply enriched by our contact with Mumia.

Our involvement, of course, was spurred on by far more than Mumia's case *per se*: our church has always spoken out against individual and state-sanctioned violence—from the treatment of Jews in Nazi Germany to the bombing of Vietnam and

Iraq. Yet even without the historical precedents, we could not have remained silent. Why? Because the life of an innocent man is at stake.

Mumia is, in reality, a prisoner of conscience. Long before his arrest in 1981—from his teen years in the Black Panther Party to his career as a radio journalist—his commitment to the ideals of honesty and fairness, and his tireless attempts to unmask the lie of governmental "justice," cost him his freedom. Tragically, they may cost him his life.

Punished most recently for writing a book—his controversial exposé *Live from Death Row*—Mumia is painfully aware of how quickly the broadest civil liberties in the world are curtailed when political power is at stake. Still, he continues to speak out. And as his fellow human beings—as his brothers and sisters—we have felt it a matter of conscience to assist him in bringing to the printed page his thoughts and feelings. In this way, from out of the sterile steel-and-block walls that isolate him, blossoms have unfolded—blossoms of thought and of spirit. Penned beneath the scribbled symbol of a flower and referred to by the silent gesture of cupped hands—wrists shackled, but palms uplifted to unfurl the fingers—they have now drifted far beyond the confines of the prison fence.

I have visited Mumia as his "spiritual advisor" for eighteen months now. There have been days when I entered the "row" depressed, weighed down with those petty problems that plague all of us at one time or another. Yet I have left again deeply refreshed and strengthened.

How is it that a wellspring of life can arise on death row? That a condemned man can speak—sincerely, even effusively—of the "wonder and joy of Life?" How is it that a despised convict, locked in a cell the size of a bathroom in the most godforsaken spot in Pennsylvania, can imbue with a spirit of freedom those who are "free?"

MUMIA IS SIMPLY A MAN. Writing to me last summer from a sweltering prison block near Philadelphia, thirteen dreadful days before his scheduled (and then suddenly postponed) execution date, his soul cries out:

> I would be lying if I told you I've not had those nights—dark nights of the soul where death itself seems welcome . . . I sometimes want to shout—"I am not a symbol; I am a man!" But on this my fabled "voice" falters. I am no more, no less, than a man—a human fighting for his breath in a shifting sea of

codified hatred. As I seek a safe shore, a harbor, I am buffeted by swells that threaten to drown out my very existence . . . For me, the "law" is not a refuge, but a ravenous great whale circling ever closer, seeking its prey.

And so he sits on death row today, his future uncertain, but his spirit still unfettered. As he writes in another letter:

. . . Loneliness is but an illusion. One man, "living" on one of the most damned sites on earth, is not truly alone. The death chambers of America are not as tightly sealed as many may suspect, for how can Spirit be kept out?

It is often said that when a writer bares his soul in a book, a small part of it travels to every reader. Here, then, from the heart and soul of Mumia Abu-Jamal to yours, are the flowers of his spirit.

New Meadow Run Bruderhof
October 1996

A Write-up for Writing

ON JUNE 3, 1995, one day after being served with a death warrant, I was served with a "write-up," a misconduct report for "engaging actively in a business or profession," i.e., as a journalist. So strongly does the state object to me writing what you are now reading that they have begun to punish me, while I'm in the most punitive section that the system allows, for daring to speak and write the truth.

The institutional offense? My book, *Live from Death Row*. It paints an uncomplimentary picture of a prison system that calls itself "correctional" but does little more than corrupt human souls; a system that eats hundreds of millions of dollars a year to torture, maim, and mutilate tens of thousands of men and women; a system that teaches bitterness and hones hatred.

1

Clearly, what the government wants is not just death, but silence. A "correct" inmate is a silent one. One who speaks, writes, and exposes horror for what it is, is given a "misconduct." Is that a correct system? A system of corrections? In this department of state government, the First Amendment is a nullity. It doesn't apply.

No one—not a cop, nor a guard—can find one lie in *Live from Death Row;* indeed, it is precisely because of its truth that it is a target of the state and its minions—a truth they don't want you to see.

Consider: Why haven't you seen, heard, or read anything like this on TV, radio, or in the papers? Newspapers, radio, and TV are increasingly the property of multinational corporations or wealthy individuals and therefore reflect the perspective of the rich and the established, not the poor and powerless.

In *Live from Death Row,* you hear the voices of the many, the oppressed, the damned, and the bombed. I paid a high price to bring it to you, and

I will pay more; but, I tell you, I would do it a thousand times, no matter what the cost, because it is right! To quote John Africa:

"When you are committed to doing what is right, the power of righteousness will never betray you. . . ." It was right to write *Live from Death Row,* and it's right for you to read it, no matter what cop, guard, prisoncrat, politician, or media mouthpiece tells you otherwise.

Bu. Jamal

Every day of your life, no doubt, you've heard of "freedom of speech" and "freedom of the press." But what can such "freedom" mean without the freedom to read, or to hear, what you want?

As you read this, know that I am being punished by the government for writing *Live from Death Row,* and for writing these very words. Indeed, I've been punished by the United States government for my writings since I was fifteen years of age—but I've kept right on writing. **You keep right on reading!**

BOOKS

A N D   T H E   S T A T E

The writer who is endorsed by the state is the writer who says what everyone wants to hear: the allowable things. It is noteworthy that even at this time in world history, those who write satire, social commentary, or works of opinion can be damned, threatened, and marked for death because of their words. Take Salman Rushdie. How many people have actually read his works? I have read *The Satanic Verses,* also *Haroun and the Sea of Stories.* I cannot speak for a Muslim, of course, yet I found him fascinating, funny, and an extremely good writer. I can understand why the state felt threatened by his work. What I don't understand is why they would think of doing something that will only immortalize it.

If there's one thing we've learned in two thousand years, it's that you cannot kill a book. One of the greatest science-fiction films I have ever seen, *Fahrenheit 451* (that's the point at which paper combusts spontaneously), which is based on a Ray Bradbury novel, portrays a futuristic society in which books are banned and people cannot hold unorthodox ideas. In this society there are subver-

sives—people who read books. The subversives
keep their books hidden in attics, in basements,
and behind false walls. And this old lady in the
film tells a young girl that she likes books and has
some hidden in her attic. Somehow the word
gets out, and when it does, the alarms start
ringing and they call the fire department. The fire brigade rushes to the
house, axes the doors, and starts
a fire: they burn the house to
the ground. Finally all the
subversives or rebels
flee the country to
a place where people
become books. In a sense,
the film tries to show how far
the state will go to ban books, or
anything it perceives to be dangerous, for that matter. But it also shows
how useless all those measures are.

You cannot kill a book.

Capital Punishment

THE DEATH PENALTY is a creation of the State, and politicians justify it by using it as a stepping stone to higher political office. It's very popular to use isolated cases—always the most gruesome ones—to make generalizations about inmates on death row and justify their sentences. Yet it is deceitful; it is untrue, unreal. Politicians talk about people on death row as if they are the worst of the worst, monsters and so forth. But they will not talk about the thousands of men and women in our country serving lesser sentences for similar and even identical crimes. Or others who, by virtue of their wealth and their ability to retain a good private lawyer, are not convicted at all. The criminal court system calls itself a justice system, but it measures privilege, wealth, power, social status, and—last but not least—race to determine who goes to death row.

Why is it that Pennsylvania's African-Americans, who make up only 9 percent of its population, comprise close to two-thirds of its death row

---

1. See Abu-Jamal, *Live from Death Row*, xvii.

population?[1] It is because its largest city, Philadelphia, like Houston and Miami and other cities, is a place where politicians have built their careers on sending people to death row. They are not administering justice by their example. They are simply revealing the partiality of justice.

Let us never forget that the overwhelming majority of people on death row are poor. Most of them cannot afford the resources to develop an adequate defense to compete with the forces of the state, let alone money to buy a decent suit to wear in court. As the O.J. Simpson case illustrated once again, the kind of defense you get is the kind of defense you can afford. In Pennsylvania, New Jersey, and New York, in Florida, in Texas, in Illinois, in California—most of the people on death row are there because they could not afford what O.J. could afford, which is the best defense.

One of the most widespread arguments in favor of the death penalty is that it deters crime. Study after study has shown that it does not. If capital punishment deters anything at all, it is rational thinking. How else would it be conceivable in a supposedly enlightened, democratic society? Until we recognize the evil irrationality of capital punishment, we will only add, brick by brick, execution by execution, to the dark temple of Fear. How many more lives will be sacrificed on its altar?

RECENTLY I CAME across words from Gibran, one of my boyhood heroes, and reflected on them as I hadn't in more than a generation. What reader of this passage from *The Prophet* can but pause for thought?

Oftentimes have I heard you speak of one who commits a wrong as though he were not one of you, but a stranger unto you and an intruder upon your world.

But I say that even as the holy and the righteous cannot rise beyond the highest which is in each one of you,

So the wicked and the weak cannot fall lower than the lowest which is in you also.

And as a single leaf turns not yellow but with the silent knowledge of the whole tree,

So the wrong-doer cannot do wrong without the hidden will of you all.

Like a procession you walk together towards your god-self.

You are the way and the wayfarers.

And when one of you falls down he falls for those behind him, a caution against the stumbling stone.

Ay, and he falls for those ahead of him, who though faster and surer of foot, yet removed not the stumbling stone.

Here I sat, on death row, of all places, and not only on death row, but on Phase II, beside men who, like me, had a few weeks left to live.

One of them, a middle-aged, frog-voiced Vietnam vet, would rather die, than live in this Hell of cells, and, refusing all appeals, did die by lethal injection; by judicial murder, by state diktat. His name was Leon Moser.

Two doors down from me, I tried to get him to fight for his life, to get him to battle the political whores who were using his life, and his very death, as stepping stones to higher political office such as elected judgeship:

"Look, man. I understand how you feel. Hell, if I was a middle-aged white dude from the boondocks stuck down here in this black 'n' Spanish village, well—hey—I might do the same thing, or feel like it. Graterford must make you feel as if you were in a foreign country.

"Also, wouldn't it be good to beat those slimy lawyers in the D.A.'s office, who owe their careers to your life—and your death? I know you hate lawyers!"

"I think lawyers are sleazy, yes. But I don't really care about being executed. As far as I'm concerned the man they sentenced to death died over ten years ago. To execute me won't mean nothing, 'cause that man ain't alive no more. To kill me, Jamal, is just like puttin' out garbage."

Moser welcomed death like a long-lost lover, and the State, thirsty for his blood, rushed him off into eternity, ignoring even the attempted telephonic intercession of a federal judge. Defense lawyers criticized his execution as a rush to death.

In those few times I saw him in that dark, humid, and stifling Phase II, Moser appeared fifteen years older than he really was; his hair more white than brown, his beard a whitened, chest-long brush, his visage a stark contrast to pictures published in the daily press, which showed a younger, browner-haired, less furtive face.

He walked with a permanent hump, as if a demon the size of a rogue elephant rode his back, bending him down, down, and still farther down.

For such a one, might not death bring the hope of a respite?

James Harris

POLITICS

PEOPLE SAY they don't care about politics; they're not involved or don't want to get involved, but they are. Their involvement just masquerades as indifference or inattention. It is the silent acquiescence of the millions that supports the system. When you don't oppose a system, your silence becomes approval, for it does nothing to interrupt the system. People use all sorts of excuses for their indifference. They even appeal to God as a shorthand route for supporting the status quo. They talk about law and order. But look at the system, look at the present social "order" of society. Do you see God? Do you see law and order? There is nothing but disorder, and instead of law there is only the illusion of security. It is an illusion because it is built on a long history of injustices: racism, criminality, and the enslavement and genocide of millions. Many people say it is insane to resist the system, but actually, it is insane *not* to.

11

The Search

LIFE HAS EVER BEEN in search of answers to basic questions—What is Life? Who is God? Why?

As a boy, this quest took me to the oddest places. When Mama dragged us to church, it seemed more for her solace, than ours. A woman who spent most of her life in the South, she must've felt tremendous social coldness up North. "Down home" was "down South," for even after over a decade, the brick and concrete jungle we walked daily didn't seem like home.

Only at church did it seem that Mama returned home. It was a refuge where women her age sought a few hours for the soul's rest while the preacher performed. In a sense, Sunday trips to church were her weekly "homegoing." They were islands of the South—its camaraderie, its rhythms, its spiritual community—come north.

Yet for myself, as for most of my siblings, church was a foreign affair. We had never lived (and seldom visited) in Mama's Southern birthland, and the raucous, tambourine-slapping, sweat-drenched, organ-pounding milieu couldn't be more alien. We weren't Southerners.

Black preachers, especially those of Southern vin-
tage, are extroverts in style, diction, and cadence.
They may yell, shriek, hum, harrumph, or sing.
Some strut the stage. Some dance. Black Baptist
preachers, especially, are never dull or monotonal.
Their sermons aren't particularly cerebral. Nor
should they be. They preach to congregations
whose spirits have been beaten down and bat-
tered all week long. To them, Sundays are thus
days when the spirit, not the mind, needs lifting.
So preachers must perform, and sermons become
exercises in exuberance.

I remember staring at the preacher—his furrowed
face shining with perspiration, eyes closed, lips
locked in a holy grimace—and wondering to myself, "What da hell did he just say?" His thick, rich,
southern accent, so accessible to Mama, was Greek
to me.

Part of me was embarrassed, but the other couldn't
give a damn. I couldn't care less what the preacher
was saying, and he couldn't care less what I was
thinking. I was thinking: I am bored to tears.

The only "salvation" I felt in church was the rap-
turous joy I felt when I looked around me. Here, I
thought, are some of the most beautiful girls in the
world.

I was lost in a reverie, in rapt adoration, my eyes
locked on a girl a few pews back. She had fresh

pressed hair; a crisp, starched dress; patent leather shoes that shone brighter than the real stuff. Her dark brown legs shimmered with the luster of Vaseline. . . .

Then a painful pluck would pull me from my rapture, and Mama's clenched lips whispered, "Boy! Turn yo' narrow behind around now! Straighten up!" I would simmer. Who would choose to stare at an old preacher when there was a pretty girl to look at? If I hadda choice between 'em—well, that wouldn't be no contest. But I was only ten. Mama made the choice for me. I turned, glowering.

It was only several years later, when I was no longer forced to go to church, that I really began to explore the realm of the spirit. Sometimes I went to Dad's church. Although Mama was a bred-in-the-bone Baptist, Dad was Episcopalian. He had taught me how to read by using the Bible, and seemed to take pleasure in listening to me read Holy Scripture.

After the raucousness of Mama's Baptist church, Dad's Episcopalianism seemed its quiet antithesis. Whereas Second Pilgrim's was cramped, Episcopal was spacious. Baptists sang and danced; Episcopalians were reserved and stately. Mama's friends shook their tambourines in North Philly. Dad's sang hymns in the foreign outlands of Southwest Philly.

Dad's church was vast, reflecting substance and wealth, yet it didn't feel like home. Maybe Mama's church was a sweatbox. Dad's seemed a cold fortress. Soon I began to seek my own spirit-refuge, going wherever I felt the spirit lead me. Like to the synagogue.

יהוה

THROUGH READING the Bible and other books, I knew that the Scriptures were supposed to be the Word of God. I thus reasoned that among the Jews, whose faith is rooted in the Old Testament, I would find this Word in a purer form. One day I went to seek it.

In North Philly's bustling black and Puerto Rican neighborhoods, Jews were a distinct and rare minority—old men, and a few women, who sold chickens, clothing, or peanuts. Their house of prayer, however, was hardly distinct: a small synagogue, it stood recessed, tucked in between the storefronts that margined it like the edges of a book cover.

Inside the vestibule, six or seven old men stood, chanting in an unknown tongue. They wore yarmulkes on their heads, and prayer shawls fastened across their chests covered their stooped shoulders. The room was dark, and what little sun seeped in hardly penetrated the dimness. Dust motes swam like goldfish in thin ribbons of filtered light. To this day, I remember the dust; the dust of old stones, of old men. And the smell of old men.

The rabbi, his eyes enlarged by bifocals, shuffled over to me, his shoulders stooped, his eyes sharp. "Can I help you, young man?" His speech was guttural, thick; colored with Yiddishisms. There seemed to be—or was I only imagining it?—an aura of fear around him stirred, perhaps, by my entrance. Who was this big, beardless youth confronting him?

As tall black men learn to do, I made myself mentally smaller, and looked askance as I explained my reason for entering the synagogue.

"Yes, sir. I—umm—I'm—umm . . . I wanna learn about Judaism."
"Vy iz dat?"
"Well, I'm interested in learning about the religion that really began Christianity."
"Vell—Vy?"
"Umm . . . becuz I think I wanna become a Jew."
"Dyou *vat?* Vat you mean? Vy dyou say *dat?*"
"Well—I'm interested in a pure religion. I've read that the Bible has been tampered with; there are

different translations and stuff. I wanna study what God really said, you know . . ."

The rabbi stared at me. He was trying to formulate an answer, but the words stuck to his tongue. I looked into his eyes and saw incredulity dueling with quiet surprise. Is he serious? silly? he seemed to be asking. Then he turned and looked around, as if searching for something.

"Vait uh minute."
"Zis vill help you, young man," he said, handing me an envelope, and walking me to the door.
"Ven you are finished, come back, ya?"
"Thank you, sir!"
"By ze vay, dyou know, zair ah black Chews. Haf you efer heard von Sammy Davis chunior?"

I nodded assent.

"Veil, he is a black Chew, you know?"

He bade me farewell. I left the Market Street Synagogue high with expectation, racing home.

Once in my room, I tore apart the thick brown envelope and found a slim, rust-colored volume bound in leather. I opened it, but stopped short in dismay. What was this? There was not one English word within its covers! It was entirely in Hebrew. Tears leapt to my eyes. The search was sure to continue.

III

MY FIRST VISIT to a Catholic church was a visit into a place of contrasts, a place where the visages in stone radiated reverence, but faces of flesh reflected unmitigated hatred.

I remember sitting in Mass, listening to the strange intonations of the priests—*Agnus Dei, qui tollis peccata mundi . . . miserere nobis*—and noticing their turned heads, faces tight with spirals of hatred, aimed at me, a lanky black youth kneeling in the white midst.

"Do they know me?" I wondered. "Why are they angry at me?"

Confusion warred with amazement: how could the House of God so plainly be a house of hatred toward one who sought the divine presence within its walls? Wasn't this the Church Universal, the Mother Church?

Although barely in my teens, I knew what I saw, and I acknowledged the feelings of the people around me. Matronly heads covered in firmly knotted scarves, these silent, solid, middle-aged Poles, Ukrainians, and Slavs (there were also a few Puerto Ricans) never said a thing, but their faces—their coldly darting eyes, and tight, wrinkled mouths—spoke to me louder than screams:

"Nigger! What are you doing in this church? *Our* church?"

Day by day, week by week, month by month, I began to ask myself that very question.

Where once the church had offered a quiet place for spiritual reflection on its catechismal mysteries, it now pulsated with resentment at my dark presence.

When I went to catechism I heard of one world; when I walked into church I saw another.

The straw of severance came on April 4, 1968, the day Martin Luther King, Jr. was assassinated. I was on my way to catechism, and as I trudged my way to the rectory, my slowing gait seemed to reflect my inner reluctance. A weight hung on my mind like an anvil.

"King believed in nonviolence—and *still* they killed him!"
"They? Who *they?*"
"White folks—white folks couldn't bear to hear him—to see him!"

My conversation with self went point-counter-point . . . By the time I got off the trolley near St. John's, my legs were leaden. I walked at a snail's pace.

Sitting down with Father to begin the lesson, he noticed my reticence.

"What's wrong, young man? You seem distracted."

"Father . . ."

"Yes, go on."

"I heard on the news today that Reverend Martin Luther King was assassinated . . ."

"I heard it too. Some of the Fathers and brothers are glad."

"Glad?"

"Yes. They saw him as a troublemaker."

"Really? Really, Father?"

"Some—not all. Especially not one of our Fathers."

"Why 'especially' not one?"

"Well—how do I put it . . . Well—one of our Fathers is half-Negro."

"Really, Father?"

"Yes. Why?"

"Do you think I could talk to him?"

"Why?"

"Well, Father—perhaps . . . maybe he can understand how I feel."

"That may be, but, uh . . . you cannot talk with him." "Why not, Father?"

"Well . . . it's a secret. I can't tell you which Father it is."

A man, a priest, ashamed of his race? I had come to catechism that night seeking peace for the tempest that raged in my soul. Now, leaving St. John's, I was more at sea than when I arrived.

All those months! A half-black priest! Ashamed of his race? Priests who were *glad* that King was killed? Where was I? What was I doing here? I wept bitter tears. Not for King—I felt he was wrong, a soft-hearted non-realist—but for my parents and all others who revered him. King was an educated preacher of nonviolence, yet to these priests he was just another nigger.

What was I doing in this place, a place that hailed his murder? If they thought that way about him, how did they really feel about me?

I cried for the loss my mother and her generation felt—the assassination of their dreams, the scuttling of their barely born hopes. I cried for the loss of a boy's faith. I cried for a nation on the razor's edge of chaos.

A BLACK NATIONALIST even in my pre–Black Panther youth, it was perhaps inevitable that my search for meaning would bring me, sooner or later, to test the waters at a local mosque. Little more than a storefront on an out-of-the-way street in South Philly, the building seemed the antithesis of all the religious sites I'd been to before. Christian and Jewish houses of worship were ornate as a rule, especially their cathedrals. This place could not have been plainer: walls painted white, with the front of the room adorned by a chalkboard that faced the assembled. There was also a flag featuring a white star and crescent in a bright field of red, with a letter in each corner: F, J, E, and I—Freedom, Justice, Equality, and Islam.

It was a summer night and midweek, so the gathering was small, yet Brother Minister, a dark-skinned man in navy suit, glasses, and bow tie who went by the name of—was it Benjamin? Benjamin X?—preached passionately. The captive audience punctuated his every sentence: "Uh-huh!" "That's it!" "Teach, bro minister! Wake 'em up!" His baritone was smooth, colored by that ubiquitous Southern accent I was to find later in almost every mosque I visited, whether north or south of the Mason-Dixon line. His message was not.

"Brotha . . . I say to you here and now, the white man is the devil! Why, when you look at how this man has stolen millions of our people from Africa, sold our mothers and fathers into slavery in the hells of North America for four hundred years; beat us, abused us, lynched us, and tortured us—well, how could any man be anything *but* a devil?"
"Uh-huh!"
"Preach it, Bro. Minister!"
"Our leader and teacher, the Honorable Elijah Muhammad, teaches us, brotha, that the devil's time is almost over!"

"That's it, brotha!"

"Wake 'em up!"

"I said, 'The devil's time is almost up!' Why, look all around the world—from Vietnam to Detroit—and you'll see the white man catching hell! Am I right, brothas?"

"That's it!"

"Uh-huh!"

Minister Benjamin X spoke for what seemed to be hours, and after his lecture, a collection was taken.

Returning home, I reflected on the similarities between my Baptist and Muslim experiences. I was struck by how the Muslim minister—though his mouth vibrated with the rhythms and cadences of the black South, and though his message was shaped in a way that spoke to my ethnic, historical, and cultural realities—sounded for the most part like a Christian in a bow-tie.

The main difference, perhaps, lay in their views of evil. Where the Baptist spoke of a metaphysical devil, the Muslim preached of a living one. I couldn't bring myself to believe that the white man was supernatural, even supernaturally evil—if anything, they were sub-naturally human, I thought to myself. Yet it seemed as improbable that they were devils, as gods. The search would continue.

Thoughts on the Divine

An interviewer once asked the Mahatma Gandhi: "Gandhi-ji, it seems that you worship sometimes in temples, sometimes in churches, sometimes in mosques. What is your own religion?" Gandhi replied: "Follow me for a few days. Watch what I do; how I walk, what I say, and how I conduct myself generally. *That* is my religion."

THERE ARE AS MANY religions as there are cultures, and equally many names for the divine presence that is the heart of each. The energizing influence of belief keeps them apart, for to each adherent they contain truth that, from his or her perspective, is the *only* truth. All the same, it seems they flow in one direction, like many streams seeking release into one mighty river.

My youthful search for meaning revealed that no matter how differently the Infinite was clothed in the garb of a certain religion, it was there. In each, I found a new perception of the greatest good, that is, a belief in God or some other personification of the divine principle. I found, as George Bernard Shaw puts it, that there is "only one religion, though there are a hundred versions of it."

In Judaism, the ancient ancestral warrior is revered as all-powerful Yahweh, or Jehovah; to Christians, the Jewish carpenter Yeshuah is God yet also Man; for the Muslim, the ancient Meccan gods find fusion in one supreme being—*Al-Lah,* the God. In Hinduism, Lord Krishna emerges from a vast pantheon of ancient deities as a blue-black god who twirls and leaps in an eternal sacred dance. To the Buddhist, the insights of Gautama Siddhartha form the central core of a faith that holds the promise of enlightenment and the discovery of the true Self. In Santería, Condoblé, and Voudoun, the ancient gods of African antiquity have survived to smile behind the faces of the Catholic saints.

In the essence of each religion, then, we see a projection of the greatest good. For a threatened, nomadic desert tribe, what greater good than the worship of a mighty and powerful ancestor, a prominent warrior—Yahweh—who defended the clans? For the maligned followers of a Nazarethan carpenter, one crucified by the mightiest Empire of the age, why not the greater good of his victory over the tomb? For contentious Arab clans who saw each other through the lens of enmity and conflict, why not the clarity and simplicity of

One God to reign over the throngs who crowd the K'aaba—One God to bring unity to a people, a region, a sphere of influence?

To Hindus, whose plethora of deistic personalities reflect the God-force that permeates all creation, Krishna—the beautiful, playful, dark boy-god who loves cattle and dances with other cowherds— turns the boring and mundane into a sacred act. For the Buddhist, Gautama's attainment of enlightenment seeks the void beyond which no personality, human nor divine, exists. It bespeaks a greater good that sees past the soul to ultimate nothingness, a spiritual place of rest.

To millions of stolen and enslaved African peasants, for whom return to the grasslands, forests, and villages of the black motherland was physically impossible, their religion was the only means of a voyage home. Under a new, cooler sky, ancient gods and honored ancestors came to life once more and provided the greater good of spiritual survival, of an inner Self that could withstand the most dehumanizing assaults and empower the soul to remain sane. Even in the midst of a powerless existence, the world of the invisible pulsed with names like Yemonja, the goddess of the river; Obatala, chief of the gods; and Shango, the god of war and thunder.

Many of our ideas about God and religions simply mirror the traditions we have inherited from
our forebears. They are imbibed with mother's
milk, openly, uncritically, freely—illogical human
expressions, exercises in irrationality. Others are
perceptions gained only by leaping into the dark
arms of faith. God comes, in various faces, and
numerous personalities, depending on our myriad
perceptions, needs, and histories. Yet if there are
any miracles left, it is that **GOD IS ONE**.

Night of Power

IN ISLAM, during the holy month of Ramadan, it is said that one night is holiest of all: *al Qadr*, the Night of Power. According to Islamic belief, it was on this night that the *Qu'ran* was delivered to the Prophet Mohammed, and it is thus the holiest of all nights. On this night, prayers are granted "for everything that matters."

The Night of Power is so deeply ingrained in the Muslim heart that a short chapter in the *Qu'ran* is devoted to it. It begins, as do all chapters therein, with the exclamation, "In the Name of God, the Compassionate, the Merciful," and goes on thus:

> Verily we have sent this
> In the Night of Power.
>
> And what will convey to you
> What the Night of Power is?

> The Night of Power is better
> Than a thousand months:
>
> The Angels and the Spirit descend in it,
> By permission of their Lord,
> For everything that matters.
>
> It is Peace:
> This until the rise of daybreak.

I will never forget the Night of Power that shook
me, not during the holy month of Ramadan, but
in the hot, humid summer of 1995, when I sat on
death row's Phase II with a date to die.

The sun had set behind the hills of West Virginia
amid ominous thunderheads, and now the forces
of nature struck like a divine assault team.

Lightning stabbed the earth as if in the throes of
celestial passion, and so powerful were the bolts
that the lights in the block—indeed, the whole
jail—flickered out.

On Phase II, lights are kept burning twenty-four
hours a day—bright during the day, dim at night—
though in fact "dim" at two in the morning is hardly
less than bright at noon. Tonight—for now at
least—it was completely dark.

I sat on the cool metal table and looked out into
the night. Cell lights, hall lights, yard lights, black

lights, perimeter lights, and lights on poles had died, and not even stars broke the black carpet. So dark!

Then: a splash of illumination that bathed the hills in blue light, a rolling boom-BOOM of thunder, and a rapid procession of blinks as lights went out all over the prison complex.

It happened again and again and again, and yet again—one sinuous bolt of lightning after the next forking the black sky, then whitewashing it to mid-day brilliance for the brief space of an eye-blink.

I sat there in the first real darkness since my arrival to Phase II, transfixed by the display of such raw, primeval power. The strikes seemed so close, I felt the hair on my arms rise.

The storm moved westward, over the prison and across the hills, and in its magnificent wake, darkness reigned as man's lights bowed their mechanical heads to the power it had unleashed.

There I sat in the darkness, with less than a month to live, yet I felt better than any other night I spent on Phase II. I felt better even than I did a few weeks later, the night my stay was granted. Why?

Then it dawned on me, like bright writing etched in my brain:

"Here is true power, my son.
See how easily it overwhelms man's 'power'?"

Watching the veins of nature pulse through the
night sea of air, making—if only for milliseconds—
daylight over the hills, I felt renewed. How puny
man seemed before this divine dance!

I saw, then, that though human powers sought
to strangle and poison me and those around me,
they were powerless. I saw that there is a Power
that makes man's power pale. It is the power of
Love; the power of God; the power of Life. I felt it
surging through every pore.

Nature's power prevailed over the man-made, and
I felt, that night, that I would prevail. I would overcome the state's efforts to silence and kill me.

America exists

in a virtual sea of materialism. Here, one sees material excess in the midst of utter poverty. Here, in the cradle of global capital power, one finds more food, more clothing, more creature comforts, more material wealth than almost anywhere on this planet.

Ironically, the lives of many surrounded by opulence are awash in unhappiness. This nation eats most of the world's food. It consumes most of the world's energy. It treats the vast lands and seas of the earth as if it were a toilet bowl. It gains its material wealth from the theft of other people's lands and the exploitation of other people's labor.

Its principle is not—and never has been—something as amorphous as "Christianity"; it is naked materialism. This materialism drives not only the elite, but average, so-called everyday folk. It forms a perspective that permeates our entire society.

Even in the realm of sexuality we are, to paraphrase the singer Madonna, material girls and boys. We define ourselves by projections, the most variant quality in human personality.

If a man is born a male, but utilizes the latest biomedical technology to transform himself into a woman, is he a woman? Or is he rather a sexual materialist who has merely purchased a new sexual persona? Are we what we look like on the outside, or are we our biological functions?

As we are with our bodies, so we are with our environment. Consciously and unconsciously, directly and indirectly, by express intent and by oblique accident, we transform the natural world toward ends we neither know nor care to know.

We rape our Mother, Earth, for new toys to play with, in order to maximize profits for men already richer than Croesus. How much is enough?

If material things are not our salvation, why do we spend our energies in endless acquisition? If wealth makes us more cruel, more calloused, and colder, what is its good?

To be sure, we live in a material universe. We must eat, and we must drink of this earth's substance. Yet after we squander its resources and make it uninhabitable, will we be able, even with our material wealth, to restore the air, to reanimate our earth, to repair the genetic damage we have done?

We are greedily eating the very heart of our tomorrow and our children's tomorrows. And meanwhile our god—the dark force of international corporate power—decides, hour by hour, how destructive the day's economic engine will be; how much long-term gain will be destroyed in the race for short-term profit.

Life's

We northerners are undoubtedly descended
from barbarian races, also in respect to our
talent for religion: we have little talent for it.

Supposing one were able to view the strangely painful and at the same time coarse and
subtle comedy of European Christianity with
the mocking and unconcerned eye of an Ep-
icurean god, I believe there would be no end
to one's laughter and amazement: for does it
not seem that one will has dominated Europe
for eighteen centuries, the will to make of
man a sublime abortion?

Friedrich Nietzsche, *Beyond Good and Evil*

ONE MIGHT be both accused and excused of
hyperbole if one were to assert that God has been
utilized to justify more human evil than has Satan.
Yet dozens of philosophers (not only Nietzsche)
have pointed out that whatever its origins and
promises, the reality of religion is this: it has often

been less a force for liberation than a tool of oppression—an impetus for civil unrest, warfare and genocide.

Wherever one stands on the religion divide, it seems clear that a new, life-affirming spirit needs expression as we end a century of carnage and move into a new millennium. Our supposedly enlightened age—the Modern Century—opened with the Boer War; it is still following the bloody path: after the Armenian massacres came the World Wars, the Holocausts of Jewish and European millions, and the atomic incinerations of Nagasaki and Hiroshima; then came Korea, Vietnam, and widespread civil war in Africa, Latin America and, most recently, Europe, not to mention the brutal repression of one small country after another by self-appointed "peacekeeping" superpowers.

If religion has had no impact on the shedding of this blood (has it done anything other than aid and abet it?) then why the need for it? How is it that we have become so numbed, that we can pretend our faith is one of resurrection and life, when in reality it serves as one of the worst flashpoints of conflict in our culture of death?

We live in a world of megadeath, on lands reddened by its original peoples, and saddened with the tears of unwilling captives. We missionize and maim, Westernize and rob, torture and starve the same fellow humans around the globe. We kill each other, but not only that; we abuse the Earth, our common mother.

We kill animals so as to be able to eat the dead. We make of our rivers, lakes, and seas, cesspools of leaden lifelessness. We pillage and burn our forests, then seek to determine why the raped earth beneath them dries into desert. We violate the mountains and line our pocketbooks with the sum of their gleaming ore. We poison our air.

Beyond the tide of materialism that encroaches our island of survival, the flood of death rises yet higher. We have attempted to mechanize, control, restrict, the very rhythms of the life process itself, and made our women's wombs into tombs. Chilled test tubes are the incubators of our perverted progress.

WHERE IS THE FAITH that truly trusts in Life? Where is the faith that seeks to bring her message to a world sliding down the slope of death? Where is the religion of Life? A religion that sets forth all the living as sacred? A religion that sees the human experience as only one paradigm in the whole connected web of nature?

Is our "God" the god of man alone? Can a Creator-God really bring into being creatures whose sole function is to serve the interests of themselves? Or is such belief really a smokescreen for our narrow schizophrenia, for the unholy greed that has brought our environment to the brink of destruction on which it now teeters? Put quite another way, do alligators live solely to be skinned for expensive shoes and luggage? Don't they—doesn't every lifeform—have an intrinsic right to exist?

It is time to recognize, as do increasing awakened numbers, that the old split-brain approach that perceives man's existence in a vacuum dooms humankind, and species uncounted, to oblivion.

We are in need of a religion of Life that sees the world in more than merely utilitarian terms. A religion that reveres all life as valuable in itself; that sees Earth as an extension of self, and if wounded, as an injury to self.

We need a religion that recognizes the interdependence of man and this world; which sees that the atmosphere surrounding our globe is the same air we breathe, and part and parcel of our lungs—that Earth's water is no different from the saliva in our mouths.

We need a religion that rediscovers the idealism that existed before institutionalism; to rediscover the primordial awe felt by ancient man when he

first beheld creation spiraling outside of his insig-
nificant self.

John Africa found such a faith and taught its simple, clear ways to others. In keeping with his natural simplicity, he called that faith Life. "Revere life,"
he taught: "Protect life, move in harmony with life."
Founding the MOVE Organization on this life-affirming principle, he imbued his followers with
an indomitable will to practice them and proclaim
them to the world.

He explained to them the worth and power of unity, the relevance and necessity of natural law, and
the meaning of resistance and rebellion against a
system bent on global self-destruction.

He taught that Earth cannot be a mere way station for the next world, to be fouled, spoiled, or
ignored.

Isn't it odd

that Christendom—that huge body of humankind that claims spiritual descent from the Jewish carpenter of Nazareth—claims to pray to and adore a being who was a prisoner of Roman power, an inmate on the empire's death row? That the one it considers the personification of the Creator of the Universe was tortured, humiliated, beaten, and crucified on a barren scrap of land on the imperial periphery, at Golgotha, the place of the skull? That the majority of its adherents strenuously support the state's execution of thousands of imprisoned citizens? That the overwhelming majority of its judges, prosecutors, and lawyers—those who condemn, prosecute, and sell out the condemned—claim to be followers of the fettered, spat-upon, naked God?

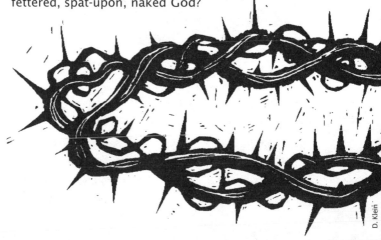

D. Klein

Spirit War

IN AN AGE when the national currency is fear, not from external threats, but from domestic ones, prisons have become places of pronounced spiritual and psychic assault. It is not surprising: as an old adage teaches, "Nothing so concentrates the mind as death." While the truism has obvious resonance to the thousands on death row, it also has its echoes for thousands more who face "life" terms. Here in morgue-like holding pens of Pennsylvania's penitentiaries, "life" literally sentences one to imprisonment for the length of one's natural lifespan, with no possibility of parole. "Life" is thus but a grim metaphor for death, for only death releases one from its shackles. "Life," it might be said, is merely slow death.

Faced with the spectral imminence of slow death, it is not unusual that for some, prison becomes a place of spiritual renewal. Often, it is men who fled religion in society at large who seek its solace in the secular hell of society behind bars. Sometimes their searches for spiritual meaning are lauded as evidence of personal progress; sometimes they are discounted as nothing but jailhouse conversions. Some may be. Others are surely not. Who can peer into the well of another's spirit?

It is not rare for a prisoner to receive, unsolicited, a religious tract from a group wholly unknown to the recipient. The pamphlet, some four to eight pages, is small—palm-sized—with biblical verses scattered throughout. "Jesus saves!" it may trumpet. Or, "Do you know where you'll be spending eternity?"

Well-intentioned as they are, prison tracts often have the opposite of their desired effect. No matter how eloquently or cleverly they purport to spread goodwill and fraternal encouragement, their essence is the same. Though they profess to care deeply about where the objects of their missionary zeal will land after death, few spare a thought for how they may spend the rest of their earthly lives. While their piety is concentrated on the Hereafter, it forgets the Here. Their writers, it seems, are so intoxicated with the thought of heaven, they are content to close an eye to the simmering hell they have helped create on earth.

They endorse, by their silence, the very systems that consign their correspondents to life-long imprisonment and scheduled death.

Often, a tract's content makes it almost impossible for the reader to escape a deeply felt suspicion that those who have sent it to him are fixated wholly on the state of his hereafter—that they couldn't give a damn about his living flesh and living soul.

IS THIS NOT STRANGE, the prisoner muses, given the spiritual adherence they claim to the teachings of a crucified God? Is it not remarkable, coming from believers of a Man-God who gave his life as divine ransom for the souls of sinners? Why is it, he asks himself, that so many Christians want to rush into a grave, those they want to *save?*

IMPRISONMENT

JUST BECAUSE your body is in prison doesn't mean your mind isn't free, and even though this thought might be trite, there is some truth in it, because we *are* our minds. In the deepest sense we are our spirits. When you think of a person, or of your own body—is not this a prison in some sense? Are we not in a prison of time? We age, we lose our faculties, but that doesn't mean we cannot overcome, and we do that by the power of mind and spirit. **We reach beyond.**

Christian? Christ-like?

For centuries in America, the term "Christian" has been virtually synonymous with "white." It was used not so much to distinguish believers from unbelievers, but civilized, light-skinned colonists from uncivilized, dark-skinned natives—the so-called primitive Africans, savage Indians, and other such heathen. It was a convenient spiritual underpinning for the sociopolitical economic order, that is, the "order" of white supremacy and domination. In such a context, the conversion of a non-white to the dominant, European faith meant next to nothing, for what did it matter what faith lived in the heart of a man, if his skin remained black or red?

Virginia's Act of 1667 was no anomaly. A similar act became law shortly afterward in South Carolina, and in another colony, an act passed in 1690 declared quite openly that "no slave shall be free by becoming a Christian." And so, new generations of Christians were baptized, and new generations of preachers, holding them in the thrall of a system that made reading the Scriptures for themselves a capital crime, continued to intone submission: "Slaves, obey your masters."

44

What did "Christianity" mean to those tens and hundreds of thousands of men, women, and children brought to our shores in shackles from the west coast of Africa? What did it mean to those hardy survivors of the dreaded Middle Passage who were forced to learn a new, foreign language and forbidden to speak their own tongue under threat of the lash? No less important, what does it mean today, to their great grandchildren, now legally free to practice the religion of their choice?

Should Afro-Americans praise the god of men who brought their forebears here in fetid, feverish holds? A god whose people wiped out all but the last vestiges of a native population? A god of invaders and slavemasters? Should anyone?

Formed in the age of Roman imperial supremacy and Palestinian servitude, Christianity became, in America, the faith of the slavemaster, the alleged belief of the rich, the protector of the propertied. For the slave, though, it was more farce than faith; in his eyes what was truly worshipped by all was wealth.

Indeed, "Christianity" became cultural shorthand for the status quo, the existing system of naked, race-based oppression. The fiction that the Euro-American conquest of the New World was motivated by efforts to "convert" indigenous peoples, or that African slavery was necessitated by a desire to bring "the gospel" to the "natives" is rebuffed by the hand of history. One need only examine the past five centuries from a native perspective—centuries that brought devastating disease, bloody persecution, rampant alcoholism, and ultimately, confinement in concentration camp–like reservations—to understand why the god of the pale-faced invaders seemed less a Great Spirit of goodness than a demon of destruction.

We have already seen above that even conversion had no real impact on the convert's state of bondage. As generations yet unborn were to remark, with a truth that resonated equally well for one of African descent as for the native American: "When the Europeans came, they had their Bible and we had our land; now, they have our land, and we have their Bible."

Did the native or the slave really expect his master to sacrifice property and power on the altar of piety? The story of the Cherokee, derisively referred to as the "White Indians," reveals a disturbing answer.[1]

In religion, education, cultural and political life, and even architecture, the Eastern Cherokee adopted European forms of life to a far greater

---

1. For documentation of Cherokee history, see John Ehle, *Trail of Tears: The Rise and Fall of the Cherokee Nation* (New York: Anchor/Doubleday, 1988).

degree than any other tribe in North America. By the early 1800s, they were building wood and brick homes; they also founded a capital, New Echota, organized a Cherokee Supreme Court, and published a newspaper in an alphabet developed by their famed linguist Sequoyah, a.k.a. George Gist.

Baptist and Moravian churches converted significant numbers to their faiths. The Cherokee were, relatively speaking at least, a wealthy people, with successful crafts and farming operations and hundreds of thousands of head of cattle, horses, and mules. So similar were they to whites that they owned a population of several thousand black slaves. Here was a tribe that was by all measurements a "civilized" tribe: it was Christian, literate, propertied, and law-abiding.

Cherokee "progress" did not come without a cost. Aside from the fact that it meant the destruction and replacement of their own indigenous culture by a European replica, it fueled the resentment of a white economic elite driven by supremacist and expansionist goals. In addition, poorer colonists agitated against their "red" competitors, and the government intervened. Before long, the Cherokee became victims of the same white greed that was to destroy every other native tribe.

Legal victory brought new hopes to the Cherokee in 1832, when they brought suit in the Supreme Court and won a judgment against Georgia, whose "Indian statutes" were declared unconstitutional and thus unenforceable. In *Worcester & Butler v. Georgia* (1832) the Court held:

> The Cherokee Nation then, is a distinct community, occupying its own territory, with boundaries accurately described, in which the laws of Georgia can have no force, and which the citizens of Georgia have no right to enter but with the assent of the Cherokees themselves or in conformity with treaties and the Acts of Congress.

Yet President Andrew "Indian Killer" Jackson refused to follow the ruling and was quoted by journalist Horace Greeley as saying, "[Chief Justice] John Marshall has made his decision; let him enforce it now if he can."

Apparently he couldn't. Already the same year, large tracts of Cherokee ancestral lands were surveyed, divided up, and assigned to white settlers by lottery. By the end of the decade, Georgia's entire Cherokee population was decimated. Evicted from their lands under force of martial "law," whole settlements were marched off to faraway Oklahoma under military escort, straggling along a wintry Trail of Tears whose hardships cost them (and their black slaves, though these were never deemed important enough to count) thousands of lives.

"Civilized" and "Christianized," the Cherokee still lost everything dear to them—their ancestral grounds, their homes and livestock, their children, their women, their elderly, their sick—all because other "Christians" wanted their land. Yet to white minds this unholy program of "resettlement" entailed no losses: it was simply another step in building the foundation on which the very existence of most southern and western states rests.

Today, the Cherokee exist only as a remnant of the past, their reservations an attraction for passing tourists. As for the descendants of Virginia's Christian slaves, they are now free, but the vast majority are still dutifully Christian. True, their churches have remained distinct from white churches in many ways. But those cultural trappings aside, one is tempted to wonder whether the black church doesn't carry the selfsame mission as its white counterpart—and whether the vision that guides it isn't the same.

Certainly there have been men and women in every generation who have raised their voices to rouse their fellow brethren from stultifying slumber. In the 1950s and 1960s, one of the more notable of these, Dr. Martin Luther King, Jr., brought a new vitality to a church that up till then had largely sought the solace of martyred silence.

King's church was crippled not only by white supremacist terrorism, however. Equally crippling was its own counsel of quietude. Even in the face of naked injustice, there were clergymen—most white, but some black—who sought to emasculate his message: "Slow down!" "Hush, don't create such a stir!" "Wait for the right time." In a time of unprecedented struggle against the beast of American apartheid, they chose to stand firm in support of the status quo, to sprinkle on the meek and the dissatisfied alike the unholy holy water of centuries.

King's legacy lives on, but it has been twisted. His name and his words have become tools in the hands of the cleverest amongst his enemies to attack, belittle, and deny the very people he sought to serve. His dreams—eloquently set to paper in speeches or essays such as *Letter from a Birmingham Jail*—have been transformed, in the mouths of the powerful, into nightmarish excuses for new chapters of negrophobia, and into attacks on those few, limited, forward steps such as affirmative action, which—if it did nothing else—was at least able to open doors previously sealed by judicial decree.

In our own time, Jean-Bertrand Aristide has noted how Haiti's history has been marked by two imperialisms, political and religious, and how the second has resulted in the development of a theology that serves only to zombify the spirit of the people in order to further subjugate them.

Jesuit scholar Ignacio Martin-Baró has used the Latin American context—in particular the bitter milieu of countries scarred by recurring civil strife—to similarly illustrate the continuing use of religion as a weapon of psychological warfare against the poor and oppressed.[2] Writing of the dueling purposes of the evangelical church and the Christian base communities in Brazil, he points out that whereas the latter have "gradually assumed a critical tendency" that questions the existing social order, the former has retained a "pentecostal posture of submission, marginalizing its converts and driving them away from any form of protest." He goes on:

> [In] the banana plantation zones of Guapiles, Costa Rica, where aggressive labor unions have traditionally held sway . . . the "Christians" (as they call themselves) not only do not join political or labor organizations but

2. Fr. Martin-Baró, five fellow priests, and their housekeepers were assassinated in November 1989 by a military death squad in El Salvador that was armed and trained by the United States.

also oppose the struggles of working people
and frequently work as scabs or strikebreak-
ers. These "Christians" have become the
banana bosses' trusted workers, and the
bosses throw all their support behind the
local evangelical churches and pressure their
workers to join them.

Writings for a Liberation Theology, 142

Clearly, no matter how long ago the stone of white
religious hypocrisy was cast into the waters of
black and native consciousness, we still live in its
ever-widening ripples.

At root, the message of the Bible is one of liberation. In the Old Testament it is exemplified by the
exodus of the Jewish slaves from Egyptian bondage; in the New, by the coming of a Messiah who
(it is promised) will save his people from the yoke
of oppression.

Until those who today call themselves "Christians"
acknowledge the carnage that has been carried out
in his name, it is hard to see how they cannot but
continue to commit deeds of devastation and evil.
In his name they go on fighting wars of avarice,
campaigns of greed, legalized land-theft, and reg-
ulated robbery; they go on firing their holy hatreds
against the rest of the world. In the very shadow of
the cross, they continue to pillage and rape. And
in the name of one who, they claim, came "to set
captives free," they continue to enslave.

Miracles

"Woe unto you that are rich,
for ye have received your consolation."

Not of a god of thunder,
a god of silk,
a god of the rich
did the carpenter speak,
but of a God of compassion,
of peace, of a day brighter
than today;

a God whose miracles still work
in the slave pens and shacks,
in the projects,
in the hellish daily life of the poor
and the oppressed—

not miracles
like walking on waves,
transforming water into wine,
but miracles of love arising
in hearts where it seems least
likely to flourish—

here and there
in the *barrios* and the *favelas,*
among those who have least,
beat hearts of hope,
fly sparks of Overcoming.

The Faith
of Slaves

The tradition of the dead weighs like a night-
mare on the brain of the living.

Karl Marx, The 18th Brumaire of Louis Bonaparte

AS IN ANTIQUITY, the black church was born in
the womb of oppression, and its adherents labored
under the heel of slavery. In a climate of general
repression, blacks (even so-called "freed" slaves)
were prohibited from a wide range of jobs and
crafts.

One area begrudgingly allowed them was that of
preacher. It was a useful allowance, for an obeisant
minister—especially one who believed in the effica-
cy of long-suffering over rebellion—could exercise
tremendous influence over his fellow captives
and save his white "Massa" countless difficulties.
Vestiges of the same attitude can be seen in a
recent controversy that surfaced during Christine
Todd Whitman's first gubernatorial campaign in
New Jersey: GOP strategists allegedly donated

considerable sums to black preachers, who in turn promised to urge their congregations to refrain from voting. (The ministers in question, of course, vociferously denied all knowledge of this.)

On the positive side, the black pulpit has been a powerful battery that energized the struggle for civil rights, and as such, other human rights movements in the late twentieth century. It is noteworthy that the most influential African-Americans of our time have been clergymen, albeit of many varied religious traditions. Dr. Martin Luther King, Jr. and Minister Malcolm X (El Hajj Malik El-Shabazz) are only two of many who come to mind.

King's influence has been reflected in the recent past in many ways, especially in the widened access blacks have gained to professions and positions previously closed to them before the passage of various civil rights laws. The influence of Malcolm X, while equally evident in the same basic realms, is also reflected in the emergence of a new and different consciousness, particularly in the Black Panther Party and many other similar black nationalist organizations across America and the black world in the 1970s.

The first, though perceived by many of his contemporaries as a radical, was at base a traditionalist whose views were largely synchronous

with the conservativism of the black church in
which he was raised. The second, known in many
circles solely for his searing revolutionary oratory,
complemented (at least in his later years) the rad-
icalism of his earlier message with a more conser-
vative spirituality colored by Arabic-influenced
Islam. Both were assassinated in the prime of
their lives as they stood on the brink of exercising
unprecedented influence on national and international affairs.

WHEREAS KING was a dyed-in-the-wool Baptist,
Malcolm X was proudly non-Christian and regarded
Christianity as a white man's religion, wielded by
slave masters to control their black chattel. He ex-
coriated the kind of Afrophobic religious thinking
described in Blyden's *Islam, Christianity and the
Negro* (1888), where the following observations are
recorded:

> It was our lot not long ago to hear an illiter-
> ate negro in a prayer meeting in New York
> entreat the deity to extend his "lily-white
> hands" and bless the waiting congregation.
> Another, with no greater amount of culture,
> preaching from John 3:2: "We shall be like
> Him," etc. He exclaimed, "Brethren, imagine
> a beautiful white man with blue eyes, rosy

cheeks and flaxen hair, and we shall be like
Him." The conceptions of these worshippers
were what they had gathered from plastic
and pictorial representations as well as from
the characteristics of the dominant race
around them.

Such psychological enslavement might seem
unbelievably blatant to us today, yet to our black
great-grandparents it was simply an expression
of a lingering self-hatred that even emancipation
could not drown from the subconscious. Its echoes
reverberate even in the present.

One example is the depiction of the deity that
continues in black churches: a white, blue-eyed
Christ peering down upon the congregation
through shimmering stained-glass windows. It
might seem like a small thing in itself, but coupled
with the undeniable fact of America's persisting
caste system, the power of suggestion it possesses
is tremendous. Perhaps it is such images that have
disenchanted and alienated many African-Americans and turned them from the churches of their
youth to the various schools of Islam, to pre-Amer-
ican or syncretic African faiths, or to the rejection
of the religious dimension of life *in toto.*

WHEN THE CHILDREN OF ISRAEL were delivered from Egyptian bondage, they traversed the desert for over forty years, until almost all those who had lived in slavery had passed away. One reading of that wilderness experience regards it as a necessary prerequisite to what was to follow: it concludes that no one with a slave psychology could live as a truly free person in the Promised Land and that, moreover, a survivor's psyche would be so indelibly etched with the taint of enslavement that it would even pose a danger to the next generation.

We who are familiar with the biblical account of the same exodus recall that, in times of peril, hunger, and doubt, a cry arose from the people, longing for the land of their oppression:

> And when Pharaoh drew nigh, the children of Israel lifted up their eyes, and behold, the Egyptians marched after them; and they were sore afraid; and the children of Israel cried out unto the Lord.
>
> And they said unto Moses, because there were no graves in Egypt, hast thou taken us away to die in the wilderness? Wherefore hast thou dealt thus with us, to carry us forth out of Egypt? *(Ex. 14:10–11)*

The Jews later mimicked their Egyptian masters by fashioning an idol in the form of a molten golden calf—an ancient example of a people adopting the religious mores of their oppressors.

In our own era and culture, the Reverend Albert Cleage created considerable controversy in Detroit when he commissioned a stained-glass montage and altarpiece for his Shrine of the Black Madonna, which featured an African Mary with an African Christ.

Not unlike the Israelites before them, it has taken generations for a once-enslaved people to reach the point of mental freedom from which they can see the face of the divine in themselves.

When the face and the presence of the divine can be glimpsed in the smile of a child—or the hope of a bride, the fecundity of a green field, the wisdom of the ancients—it is a small sign that a people are emerging from the dark coffin of bondage.

Hope

Jennifer Beach

What keeps me alive?

My belief—my religion, which I call Life—the teachings of John Africa and the example of my MOVE brothers and sisters across the state, many of whom have survived imprisonment for years and years. Their example has buoyed me up over fourteen years behind bars. Also, my faith in the power of commitment, in the power of family, in the power of love, of community, of God. I could give you one term instead of four or five. "Family," for example, means unity, commitment, love. That is "family." The other thing, of course, is laughter. Very simply, it's human to laugh and to find humor, even in something small. Every day. Every day there is *something* to laugh about! That keeps me human.

Fritz Eichenberg

SALT OF THE EARTH

Blessed are they
who are persecuted
for righteousness' sake;
for theirs is
the kingdom of heaven.

Blessed are ye,
when men revile you
and persecute you,
and say all manner of evil
against you falsely,
for my sake.

Rejoice,
and be Exceedingly glad,
for great is your reward in heaven:
for so persecuted they
the prophets before you.

Ye are the salt of the earth;
and if salt loses its savor,
of what use is it?
It is good for nothing
but to be cast out
and trodden underfoot.

Jesus of Nazareth (Matthew 5:10–13)

IT DOES NOT TAKE a biblical scholar to see that the righteous have indeed been persecuted throughout history. The "meek" may well one day "inherit the earth," yet for the last few millennia it has been the exclusive property of those in power, whilst the meek have inherited the grave.

American history provides plenty to illustrate the point: as an unsurpassed disinheritor of aboriginal peoples, it is an imperialistic nation-state composed primarily of stolen or forcibly seized territories. Were the so-called founding fathers meek, that they should inherit this piece of earth?

Central to the question is the proposition that America is a Christian nation—a nation composed of men and women eager to be persecuted for righteousness' sake. If this be so, then it is Christian to wipe out whole native peoples and commend their ravaged remnants to barren reservations; it is Christian to steal millions of people from their overseas homelands and hold them in bondage for centuries; it is Christian to cast thousands of Japanese into concentration camps and to seize their properties on the pretext of that magical word "security." If it is really so, then it is Christian to vaporize hundreds of thousands of fellow humans by dropping an atomic bomb on them, as a global "demonstration" of power; Christian to cage millions and execute thousands; Christian to devise a socio-economic system that marginalizes the weak, the awkward, the inarticulate, the down-trodden poor. Or are we to conclude that perhaps America is not a Christian nation after all?

For those faceless, nameless, black brown, and yellow millions who have been savaged by America, it might even appear that the course of its history has been guided by some demonic orientation. Instead of Christ, perhaps Dracula should be substituted for this nation's guiding god—for has it not sucked the blood of the planet's other peoples for two centuries? Does it not do so now?

Where is the God of the poor, the powerless, the damned, the crushed? Where, in national political life, is even one voice of Christ-like compassion heard?

The Roman historian Tacitus described the first Christians as a "sect" who entered his city "clad in filthy gabardines" and "smelling of garlic," a people of poverty, the salt of the earth. How, we must ask, did they come from that to this: from a tribe of the lowly to the vampires of the planet?

In order to trace the devolution, we must begin by admitting that a second crucifixion of Christ has taken place, not by a second Roman empire, but by the very men and women who bear his name: his Church.

community

Revolution is not a *word* but an *application;*
it is not *war* but *peace;* it does not *weaken,*
but *strengthens.* Revolution does not cause
separation; it generates *togetherness.*

John Africa, *Strategic Revolution*

Never doubt that a small group of committed
people can change the world; indeed, it's the
only thing that ever has.

Margaret Mead

FOR MILLIONS, perhaps billions of us, life is a
search, a journey of seeking for that which we
found unfulfilled in our youth. We search for love;
we search for family; we search for community.
And in so doing, we seek the completion of Self in
others, in the larger Self where similar selves are
united in commonality—in community.

As we search and grow, we find that modern life,
with its bursting balloons of materialism, leaves us
more and more empty inside; "things" that once
seemed to fill us now fail to bridge the gaping
chasms in our psyche. Our inner selves are pulled
in too many ways at once—the demands of work
here, and social obligations there, the pressures
of financial need (or the lesser burdens of wealth),

public responsibilities, the needs and wants of our private sphere—and finally they break, atomized, meaningless.

The dominant societal ideology of the hour is a perverse individuality hammered into our consciousness by myth and legend. It ignores the historical verity of community—of groups striving to move the social order forward. It ignores the reality that people working together are the only viable solution to any social problem.

As human beings, we are at root social creatures. Outside the bonds of our familial and social relations, we cannot truly live. Our very sanity depends on them. We are birthed in and into community. We grow in community. Community determines who we are. It is not the individual self *per se,* but its place in the broader social network of human society that defines our identity and gives our life meaning.

Whether in religious, political, economic, or educational matters, collectivity is a basic requisite for meaning. Can there truly be a religion of one? What political action can be effectively undertaken by a lone person? Doesn't every step toward economic progress require at least some level of social agreement—some willingness to put aside antagonisms—for it to function? Doesn't education,

especially as it is presently constituted, consist
largely of teaching youth how to play by the rules
of the broader social order? Is it purely coincidental
that students are organized into "classes"? Doesn't
it teach them how to acquiesce, not how—or even
whether—to transform the status quo?

And what of a circumstance in which the status
quo is unfair or oppressive? Such can be said to
have given rise to a community of resistance,
known as the MOVE organization, which, in the
words of its legendary founder John Africa, has as
its *raison d'être* total liberation:

> The MOVE organization is a powerful family
> of revolutionaries, fixed in principle, strong
> in cohesion, steady as the foundation of
> a massive tree. A people totally equipped
> with the profound understanding of simple
> assertion, collective commitment, unbending
> direction.

> While the so-called educators talk of love,
> mouth the necessity for peace, we live peace,
> assert the power of love, comprehend the
> urgency of freedom. The reformed world
> system cannot teach love while making
> allowances for hate, peace while making
> allowances for war, freedom while making
> allowances for the inconsistent shackles of

enslavement. For to make allowances for
sickness is to be unhealthy; to make con-
cessions with slavery is to be enslaved; to
compromise with the person of compromise
is to be as the person you are compromising
with.[1]

John Africa founded and forged a remarkable
family, a small but potent community of resistance
that took Life as its creed and fought to protect the
lives of all the living, even animals like dogs and
cats.

Everyone is born into the family of their flesh; here
was one of choice, commitment, and faith. It was a
family embattled, but a family nonetheless. It lives,
grows, and thrives today. Long live John Africa's
revolutionary family!

---

1. "On the Move: from the Writings of John Africa," *Philadelphia
Tribune,* 28 June 1975, 17.

Men of the Cloth

Pam Africa, minister and disciple of the teaching of John Africa, tells the true tale of a meeting between the latter and a man of the cloth behind the old headquarters of the MOVE Organization in the Powelton Village section of West Philadelphia.

The scene: a man, middle-aged, bearded, booted and blue-jeaned, is called to the back door by the leader of a small group from a nearby church. Though both are black, they present a fascinating tableau of difference. The one wears a T-shirt, sweat soaking his breast; the other is impeccably dressed in silk suit and tie, the only touch missing is coattails. The one's hair is rough, gray-fringed, uncombed, and hanging like ropes to his shoulders; the other's is pomaded, greased and brushed smooth—the head of a preacher-man.

The air is thick and charged with controversy, for the city is threatening to remove MOVE from their property and the neighborhood after a series of highly publicized confrontations with the police that has left several MOVE men and women beaten and bloody, and one MOVE baby dead.

"So, you're sayin', all I gotta do is pray, and everything
will be all right?"

"That's what I'm saying, brotha."

"If I pray, the cops will stop beatin' up my people?"

"Yes! That's what I'm saying, brotha."

"If I pray the cops will stop killin' us?"

"Yes! Pray—in Jesus name, brother—'cause the Bible
say, 'Ask, and it shall be given unto you.' That's it,
brother."

"And if I pray, our people will truly be free?"

"Uh-huh. Yessir, brother!"

"Well, c'mon, Reverend. Let's pray then."

John Africa drops to his knees, oblivious of the soft
mud already staining his jeans.

"Whoa! Whatcha doin', brotha?"

"You said we needa pray, right?"

"Uhh . . . uhh. . . ."

"Come on, Rev, pray with me, okay?"

"I . . . I . . . I meant, pray in the church."

"Why, Reverend? Ain't God out here in the open air,
ain't God all around us? Come on! Let's kneel down
here on God's earth and pray."

At this point the Reverend backs up, and John Africa
says, "What's the matter? I thought you said we
should pray. Well, come on down here and pray with
me."

The Reverend continues to stand there, staring. John

Africa asks again, "What's the matter, man? That suit you got on more important than God? I thought you said you believed in God. This dirt *is* God, so why don't you kneel down here and pray with me?"
"Well, uh . . . excuse me, brotha, but I gotta be getting back to my church."

At this point the people standing around the two men begin to speak: "You see that? That man is down there on his *knees* in the dirt; he *got* to be for real. That Reverend ain't nothin' but a phoney. He scared he gonna dirty his suit. He talkin' 'bout how he believe in God. He don't believe in nothin' but that suit."

One woman comments to another, "That preacher's a hypocrite. See, that's why I don't go to church, cuz I don't believe in them preachers, cuz they ain't nothin' but liars; they ain't for real. That man there kneelin' in the dirt *is* for real."

John Africa goes on, "You don't wanna pray with me, then, Rev?"
"I gotta go, man, uhh . . . I'm sorry."
"Why you leavin', Rev?"

The dashing preacher beats a hasty retreat from the muddy yard, more intent, it seems, on saving silk than souls. . . .

Several years later, and several miles westward, the city would torch MOVE's home and headquarters with a helicopter-borne firebomb, incinerating John Africa and ten other "longhairs" (some of them women and children) in a massacre plotted to take place on Mother's Day.

The scene: smoldering remains of an entire neighborhood, only hours before the site of a blistering, billowing inferno. Philadelphia's men of the cloth have gathered once again, though only to examine the carnage—not to weep for the fallen, nor to pray for the dead.

They have come bedecked in robes and collars, the purpose of their gathering to pray in support of the mayor of a city that has bombed its own citizens, and obliterated, incinerated, and dismembered its own babies.

The police commissioner, the fire chief, the mayor, and his officers are almost to a man "Christian"— Baptists or Catholics, most of them—religious people. Yet these men who have gathered to pray are not only churchgoers. They are ministers, pastors, priests! Aside from praying, though, it seems that they mean to do little. Why should they? They've just winked at a full-scale war waged over mere misdemeanors: at the deaths of eleven people blasted by a sky-bomb, the destruction of dozens of homes, and the permanent scarring of a neighborhood.

And so they pray and leave for home, their duties fulfilled. Men of the cloth, yes. But men of the spirit?

Hate's Unkind Counsel

A COOL AUTUMN WIND blew through the chain-link fence and razor-wire cages. Rog, a brilliant jailhouse lawyer, and I were running around in leftist circles warming up for a few games of cage handball. We had scarcely hit twenty laps when a mustached man in a sweater appeared. My counselor. We threw some words at each other, but I kept running. My jogging back faced him, moving away step by step.

"Jamal! Anything you wanna talk about? No rap, huh?"

He walked away, scribbling *pro forma* notes on his clipboard. Rog stopped running.

"What's up, man?"
"Did you see that shit, man?"
"What? Whatchu talking 'bout, Rog?"
"How that dude was lookin' atcha!"
"Whatchu mean, man?"
"Jeezus H. Kee-rist! Didn't ya see how your counselor was lookin' atchu? Talkin' to ya, Mu?"
"Hey, look, man. I don't pay that guy no mind, man."
"That's your *counselor!*"
"That's his title, but what can he do? Can he help me even get a phone call?"

"No, but—"

"See?"

"But that's not the point."

"What *is* the point, then?"

"How that dude was lookin' at you!"

"Whachu sayin', Rog?"

"That dude hates your guts, Jamal!"

"And—?"

"I jus' never saw a counselor treat a man like that.
How's it make you feel?"

"To be honest, Rog, I never really thought about it.
It's jus' normal, I guess."

"Normal? *My* counselor don't talk to *me* like that!
I looked at that dude's face, and it made my skin
crawl, Mu!"

"Really?"

"No shit, man."

I flashed in memory at his visage, and saw—*really*
saw—what upset Roger so. Here was a face of naked hatred. Why hadn't I seen it before? How had I
ignored it?

Roger, a man with three first-degree murder
convictions, three death sentences and ages beyond of time, was no Pollyanna. How could he be
so profoundly shocked at what I couldn't even see
without his help?

It dawned on me then that I *had* seen my counsel-
or's tight mask of hatred before, when he wore his

gray guard's uniform, wooden club gripped in a tight white fist, a leather thong stretched across its back.

Now that he was a counselor, his uniform had changed, but his face hadn't.

I remembered him escorting naked men to the shower, weapon in hand.

To me, he was hardly a man from whom one sought counsel, for his weapon had merely been transformed into an ink pen and a clipboard; he was an agent, albeit with another function, of the same state that fought to steal my life. And even if I had not recognized his hatred at first, I knew intuitively that there was a profound distinction between the way he saw Rog, and saw me—one I couldn't allow myself to see, but which a white death row prisoner couldn't ignore. Both of us were sentenced to death (one of us thrice!), yet one of us he treated as a man; the other as a non-human beast.

Perhaps I had subconsciously chosen to ignore the distinction before; chosen *not* to see what there was to see every day: a psychic spittle of hatred, fear, and alienation splashed against my inner person. More than choice, though, my willed blindness, pretended invisibility, and psychological self-distortion were mechanisms of self-defense: a survival stratagem in a House of Death.

Human Beings

NINETY-FIVE PERCENT of the guards I've met are doing their job simply because they need the money. Like cops and sheriffs, they are men, human beings, and their central concerns, needs, and fears are the same as anyone else's—they need money to pay rent, put bread on the table, provide an education for their children. But they have become part of the system because of their fear; they have bought into it because it is built on fear. Remember, the *system* is not a true reality, but an idea which can be fought and dismantled. People forget that we don't need the system, or the accessories we mistakenly assume are essential for living. We need only the things God gave us: love, family, nature. We must transform the system. That's the challenge. It's do-able, but only if we ourselves do it.

The Spider

NORMAN CALLED OVER, his voice heavy and strangely conspiratorial. "Hey, Mu. Ya bizzy, man?"

"Naw, Norm. I wuz jus doin' a little readin'. But wussup, man?"

"I been lookin' at this mama spider in my cell. She beautiful, man!"

"Yeah?"

"She tiny, but she so strong, man!"

"Uh huh. . . ."

"An' ya know what's amazin'?"

"Whut's dat, Norm?"

"Think 'bout how she make her own home—her web—out of her own body!"

"That's amazin', man."

And indeed it *was* amazing, especially to Norman, a man encaged in utter isolation. Here he sat—would sit for the remainder of his days—in the antiseptic stillness of a supermaximum–security prison block, yet he was not entirely alone. With a quiet, unwitting bravado that defied the state's most stringent efforts to quarantine him, spiders had moved in and built webs in the dark corner under his sink. Now they shared his cell, and he spent hours watching them spin their miraculous silken thread.

Norman watched them give birth. He watched them stalk those few rare flies who entered his cell, only to be trapped. He watched them suck the life sap from their prey until nothing remained but dry husks. He watched them in a deep and reverent wonder, and his cell became a study.

Norman watched, and whenever something truly remarkable occurred, he quietly tapped on the wall. He'd begin in a deep stage-whisper: "Mu—Yo, Mu! Ya bizzy, man?"

I was rarely too busy to listen for fifteen or twenty minutes, and it wasn't long before I found myself sharing his fascination and enthusiasm. And in time, lo and behold, a web scaffold appeared in my own sink-corner.

IN ANCIENT AFRICAN and West Indian folklore, the mother spider—Anansi—looms large. She is a wise and protective being who knows proverbs and possesses the gift of prophecy.

A famous Ghanian tale tells of a fire raging in a forest. As the beasts scamper for safety, an antelope feels a tickling sensation. A small dark spider has alighted on her ear. Before she can toss her head to flick it off, however, the spider whispers, "It is I, Anansi. Take me with you—I will repay you." The antelope, more concerned with its own survival than the minor inconvenience of a spider, agrees and runs on to safety, her path directed by Anansi.

Once she reaches safety, Anansi climbs off, thanking the antelope and promising her she won't be forgotten. Several seasons later, the antelope finds herself and her offspring threatened again, this time by hunters. Her little one is too young to run, so she instructs it to drop to the ground and hide itself in the shrubbery. Then, leaping from the undergrowth, she distracts the hunters and leads them away from her baby. Arrows whiz through the air, but the antelope is too swift. Finally the hunters give up the chase and leave the forest.

Cautiously, she returns to find her young one, whose faint cry she hears but cannot place. Where is her baby? Try as she might, she can't find her.

Just then, Anansi lets herself down from a tree limb on her slim silken cord, and announces her presence. Whispering to the mother antelope, she directs her to a clump of shrubs where, hidden under a tightly woven protective net, lies her baby. "I told you I wouldn't forget you," Anansi reminds her.

FOR NORMAN, the target of a hunt no less deadly than that of an antelope in the jungle, Anansi was vital company. In a cell constructed to maximize human loneliness—a site designed to kill the mind

—Anansi was a source of friendship and wonder. In a concrete tomb erected to smother men to death, she was a tiny, marvelous reflection of life. She brightened a man's day, and made it meaningful. Nature amid the unnatural.

The Fall

Each year, when summer fades and the air cools,
a sense of sadness pervades.
Leaf life readies its swan dive of
separation from mother tree in
an explosion of color; flowers
shrivel, and the sound
of insect life dies
away; even sweet
birdsong pales.

The earth, like an old
woman, prepares for death.
She covers herself often with
snow, and sunfire leaves her
face. Her hair, once green
and lush, thins and falls;
her blood, her blue puls-
ing blood, slows to a trickle and
eventually freezes still. All the markers of death
gather around her like a storm.

Who can but grieve? Only the certainty of renewal mitigates the pervasive sense of loss:
the knowledge that behind the cold night lies
the spring morn; that beneath fallowed earth
lies a mighty heart athrob with life; that life
lives within life, and goes forever on.

Children

IN JONATHAN KOZOL'S BOOK *Amazing Grace,* he demonstrates something of very positive significance: the power of a child's hope. The children whose stories he tells live in the worst possible conditions in the world—in drug-ridden slums—yet they still have an innate hope.

There is of course, a negative part to it that remains despite this hope, and that is the reality of the world around them. The children have hope, but they are not blind to the fact that they are often ignored, and sometimes even scorned, by the social order.

There's a little boy, David, in the book, who tells Kozol that he saw the mayor of New York City on TV, and he says, "I don't like him." Kozol asks, "Why do you say that?" And David says, "Because when I look in his eyes, all I see is coldness. He doesn't understand how poor people have to live." That is the way that most politicians in the system, actually most wealthy people, look at poor children. And the children see this; they sense this coldness coming from the people who literally control their circumstances—the conditions of the neighborhood, the state of their education.

Still, many of these children don't give up. Perhaps the best thing we can do for them is to nurture their hope—give them reason for new hopes, and feed the hope already within them so it can grow into something strong that will sustain them through life. Elie Wiesel says that the greatest evil in the world is not anger or hatred, but indifference. If that is true, then the opposite is also true: that the greatest love we can show our children is the attention we pay them, the time we take for them. Maybe we serve children best simply by noticing them.

Children do not only have an innate hope; they *are* hope. And more than that: they are our future. As Kahlil Gibran writes, they are like "living arrows sent forth" into infinity, and their souls "dwell in the house of tomorrow. . . ." They carry their hope with them to a future we can't see.

Children come to us fresh from the divine source, from what I call "Mama," from life itself, and they lead us to the same: to the God-force within creation. That is why none of us—no matter our race, creed, religion, or politics—can look at a child and not feel joy. We look at them, and something thrills us to the depth of our hearts. They are living miracles, and when we see them we know that there is a God, that life itself is a miracle. Children show us, with their innocence and clarity, the very face of God in human form.

The Creator

People have different names for God, and we
can't be offended by that. We have to try and
understand what they mean. You call him God. I
call him Mama. I see God like you see your Mama.
The closest relationship there is on earth is the
relationship between child and mother. Mama
feeds us. Her sun warms us, and her earth gives us
food; she provides air, water, pretty flowers in the
fields, trees, forests, little birds—she is Life. Life
gives life to everything in creation. That, for me,
is God. Anyone who studies religion to any depth
will find that there is a great cultural and tradi-
tional breadth in how people perceive the
divine personality. Much of it is colored
by social mores, some of it even by
politics. People are different. But
remember, all the thousands
of different names we use
for the Creator are
man-made, and the
Creator is One.

Father Hunger

IT HAS BEEN OVER THREE DECADES since I have looked into his face, but I find him now, sometimes hidden, in the glimpse of a mirror. He was short of stature, shorter than I at ten years, fully, smoothly bald, with a face the color of walnuts. He walked with a slight limp, and smoked cigars, usually Phillies. Although short, he wasn't slight, but powerfully built with a thick, though not fat, form. His voice was deep, with the accents of the South wrapped around each word, sweet and sticky like molasses.

Often his words tickled his sons, and they tossed them among themselves like prizes found in the depths of a Crackerjack box, words wondrous in their newness, their rarity, their difference from all others.

"Boys! Cut out that tusslin', heah me?" And the boys would stop their rasslin', their bellies near bursting with swallowed, swollen laughter, the word vibrating *sotto voce* in their throats: "Tusslin' —tusslin'—tusslin'—tusslin! Tusslin'!" For days— for weeks—these silly little boys had a new toy and, with this one word, reduced each other to teary-eyed fits of fall-on-the-floor laughter. "Tusslin'!"

He was a relatively old man when he seeded these sons, over fifty, and because of his age, he was

Thomas Filmyer/WCB

openly affectionate in a way unusual for a man of his time.

He kissed them, dressed them, and taught them, by example, that he loved them. He talked with them. And walked and walked and walked with them.

"Daaad! I wanna riiide!," I whined.

"It ain't good for you to ride so much, boy. Walkin' is good for ya. It's good exercise for ya."

Decades later, I would hear that same whine from

one of my sons, and my reply would echo my
father's.

His eyes were the eyes of age, so discolored by
time they seemed blueish, but there was a perpet-
ual twinkle of joy in them, of love and living. He
lived just over a decade into this son's life, and his
untimely death from illness left holes in the soul.

Without a father, I sought and found father figures
like Black Panther Captain Reggie Schell, Party
Defense Minister Huey P. Newton, and indeed, the
Party itself, which, in a period of utter void, taught
me, fed me, and made me part of a vast and
militant family of revolutionaries. Many good men
and women became my teachers, my mentors,
and my examples of a revolutionary ideal—Zayd
Malik Shakur, murdered by police when Assata was
wounded and taken, and Geronimo Ji Jaga (a.k.a.
Pratt) who commanded the Party's L.A. chapter
with distinction and defended it from deadly state
attacks until his imprisonment as a victim of frame-
up and judicial repression—Geronimo, torn from
his family and children and separated from them
for a quarter of a century.

Here in death row, in the confined substratum of
a society where every father is childless, and every
man fatherless, those of us who have known the
bond of father-son love may at least re-live it in our
minds, perhaps even draw strength from it. Those

who have not—the unloved—find it virtually impossible to love. They live alienated from everyone around them, at war even with their own families.

Here in this man-made hell, there are countless young men bubbling with bitter hatreds and roiling resentments against their absent fathers. Several have taken to the odd habit of calling me "Papa," an endearment whose irony escapes them.

It has never escaped me. I realize that I live amidst a generation of young men drunk not only with general loneliness, but with the particular, gnawing anguish of father-hunger. I had my own father; later I had the Party, and Geronimo; Delbert, Chuck, Mike, Ed, and Phil; Sundiata, Mutulu, and other oldheads like myself. Who have they had?

Yet for a long time I resisted the nickname. I resented being "Papa" to young men I didn't know, while being denied—by decree of state banishment —the opportunity to be a father to the children of my own flesh and heart. My sons were babies when I was cast into this hell, and no number of letters, cards, or phone calls can ever heal the wounds that they and their sisters have suffered over the long, lonely years of separation.

I was also in denial. For who was the oldhead they were calling? Certainly not me? It took a trip, a trek to the shiny, burnished steel mirror on the wall, where I found my father's face staring back at me, to recognize reality. I am he . . . and they are me.

Mother-loss

RELATIVELY TALL, mountainous cheekbones,
dimples like doughnuts, and skin the color of
Indian corn, she left life in the South for what was
then the promised land, "up Nawth." Although she
lived, loved, raised a family, and worked over half
her life "up Nawth," the soft, lyrical accents of her
Southern tongue never really left her. Words of
a single syllable found a new one in her mouth,
often rising on the second syllable: "Keith" became "Key-eath;" "child" became "Chy'ile," and
her reedy, lengthy laughter lit up the room
like a holiday. She, and her children, lived in
the "peejays" (the projects), but it wasn't until years later (when we were grown) that we
understood we had lived in poverty, for our
mother made sure our needs were met. She
was a gentle woman who spoke well, if at
all, of most folk, but she was like a lioness
when one of her children was attacked.

In the early 1960s, when her daughter
got caught up in a neighborhood fracas
that boiled out of control, she snapped a
broomstick in two, whipped open a path
down the block to where her daughter
stood paralyzed by terror, grabbed her,
and whipped her way back home. Only when

she was safely back indoors did she realize that
she had been slashed while outdoors—she never
noticed, so powerful was her love for her daughter.
Deep rivers of loving strength flowed through her.

A mother's love is the foundation of every love: it
is the primary relationship of all human love, the
first love we experience and, as such, a profound
influence on all subsequent and secondary relationships in life. It is a love that surpasses all
reason.

Perhaps that's why I thought she would live forever—that this woman who carried me, my brothers,
and my sister, would never know death. For thirty
years she smoked Pall Malls and Marlboros, yet
still I thought she would live forever. When she
died of emphysema while I was imprisoned, it was
like a lightning bolt to the soul. Never during my
entire existence had there been a time when she
was not there. Suddenly, on a cold day in February,
her breath had ended, and her sweet presence, her
wise counsel, was gone forever.

To know one's mother dead, yet remain imprisoned! To imagine her lifeless form while held in
shackles! To crush the hope of ever again embrac-
ing she who birthed me!

Meeting with a Killer

In Philadelphia, Hank Fahy's name is mud.

Convicted of the 1981 rape-slaying of a girl-child and subsequently sentenced to death, Fahy has dwelt in a virtual netherworld beneath the "usual" hell that is death row. Marked as a baby rapist, he has had to withstand the loathing and contempt of the many who regard his crime as an act beneath contempt.

Fahy's odyssey into the underworld has not been an easy one: bouts of suicide attempts have alternated with periods of an almost manic evangelical fervor, a living pendulum swinging between visions of hell and heaven, both just beyond his grasp.

In late June, 1995, while under his second death warrant, and with a date to die in July, Hank would come face-to-face with the living personifications of his demons and his angel.

Even while under an active death warrant, with a date to die within two weeks, Fahy was transferred to a Philadelphia city prison (rather than the state prison at Graterford, as is customary).

When he arrived, he was placed in a cell where the words "Jamie Fahy—Rest in Peace" were scrawled across the wall: Jamie Fahy, a beautiful, troubled, love-starved young girl—beaten, murdered, and al-legedly raped—Hank's eighteen-year-old daughter, who was barely four when he entered Hell.

There is more.

From impish whisperings of those around him, he learned an astonishing thing—that the man charged with beating, killing, and raping his daughter was there—not merely in the same prison —but there—on that very block!

As if inevitable, Hank met Mark (not his real name), and the hatred kindled over months melted into rare compassion.

"I hated him, Jamal," Fahy confided, "but when I saw this kid, eighteen years old, I realized what a hell he was in for; and also, I thought about the pain I would be causing his mother if I took some-thing and stuck him."

In every prison in America, murder is no mystery. There are men on death row across the nation awaiting execution for killings committed in prison.

Hank had two weeks of life left. What did he have to lose?

"You know, Jamal, I looked at this eighteen-year-old kid, and I remembered the look on my mother's face when she was alive, when she came to visit me; the shame of seeing her son on death row;

and I didn't have the heart to tell this kid, but I could see his mother lookin' at him the same way, and it hurt me, Jamal, it really did, man."

"What hurt you, Hank? Whatchu mean?"

"Well, it was two things. First, this was a set-up; I was 'sposed to kill this kid! Why else would they put us on the same block? Come on, man. Second, the same people that put me on death row are gonna put this kid on death row, but he don't know it yet."

"What did you tell Mark, man?"

"I told him 'I forgive ya, man', and I told him to let his lawyer know this, and anything I can do to help him and to keep him off death row, I'll do."

"How did you feel tellin' that boy that, Hank?"

"Ya know, Jamal, I felt good. I felt like the better man, 'cause the same system that plans to kill me, that plans to kill him, that same system that set us *both* up (for me to kill him and for him to get killed), can't do what I did—forgive."

"I loved Jamie, Jamal. She was my heart. But me killin' that kid can't bring my daughter back, and ya know what else, Jamal?"

"What's dat, Hank?"

"I wouldn't wish this—death row—on my *worstest* enemy."

N. Ascencios

Dialogue

IN OUR COUNTRY alone there are over a million men and women—not even counting juveniles—in prisons. There are an estimated three million homeless people. Poverty is widespread, and fear is the national currency. People seek the security of love, yet at the same time they are isolated, alienated—even from themselves. Isolation and alienation are barriers, forces of division. What shatters these barriers is dialogue.

Even in a free democracy, the state always attempts to control dialogue—to decide for its own interests the limits of allowable discourse. In order to be heard, one must have wealth, power, influence, rank. It's the same with the media. The media always quotes the same roundtable of "experts." Where are the voices of the poor, the excluded, the powerless? Absent those voices, absent a recognition of their worth, there can be no true dialogue, and thus no true democracy.

Objectivity and the Media

OBJECTIVITY IN JOURNALISM is an illusion, a hollow word, yet it becomes so real to its perpetrators, who have been poisoned with the lie from the first day of journalism school, that they end up not only believing in it, but letting it form the whole foundation of their profession. It's always been a great ideal, but in reality it's a misguided belief. And they end up using it to justify everything they do.

When you look at the news today—I'm talking now about national network newscasts—it is astounding that what used to make the local news, if that, is now considered as having national importance. Local crime stories, especially the most lurid ones, become national news stories not because of anything extraordinary about them, but because that is the stuff that sells. It's the old jingle: "If it bleeds, it leads." They don't feed the public pieces that stimulate intelligent thought, pieces that might make people talk or even ask questions about the fundamental relationships of power, rank, and status in this country. They're more interested in sensation.

It's almost as if the average newscast has been reduced and molded to fit *Hard Copy* or some other such show like that. The end product is trash, but it is trash that has been carefully designed to attract you emotionally, to touch you sensationally, to get you looking (but not thinking). It doesn't provoke you or encourage you to question the fundamentals. The real issues behind a story are often ignored. They're not considered important enough to be raised. That's why many people—not only MOVE, but other groups who are misunderstood and misrepresented—share MOVE's "f.t.p." attitude toward the media: Fuck the press!

By the 1970s, people began to admit that the media was in the hip-pocket of big business. Well, today the media *is* big business. The major media organizations are not just controlled by it—they are part of it. Many of them are owned by huge multinational corporations. And if you think they don't control what comes over the air, you're in for a surprise. If I control your paycheck, I tell you what to say and what not to say.

When Rizzo was mayor, he was always taking the Philadelphia media to task and—especially during the time of the 1978 MOVE confrontation—accusing them of stirring things up with their advocacy journalism. They lacked objectivity, he complained.

Francis Jetter

Well, Rizzo was right on one count, because, as I said earlier, journalistic "objectivity" is non-existent. Who's objective? But as far as the slant of their advocacy goes, I don't know who Rizzo thinks they were advocating. It sure wasn't MOVE.

Neither the brutal police assault on the MOVE compound in August 1978 nor the bombing of their new compound in May 1985—in which eleven of their members were killed, and a whole neighborhood was destroyed—could ever have happened without the media. It was in their interest to create the fires of carnage and hatred, and feed those fires. The media built the scaffolding around the MOVE standoff, and the information they disseminated became the catalyst for the final conflagration. The next step after that was for them to whitewash the whole thing to save face for the "investigative" commission.

The frightening thing is that the press's involvement in the MOVE debacle was in no way unique; it is instructive for the present, the future, and for any number of contexts and loci, not just racist Philadelphia. Don't forget—two things always define the media's perspective: money and power. And the resulting "blindness" is therefore often willful.

I remember being down in Philadelphia at my petition hearing in the fall of 1995—I was being shuttled back to the prison, and the sheriff had turned the radio on. The newscaster was announcing that ABC had just been acquired by the Disney Corporation. I laughed. I was in the back of the van laughing and laughing and thinking to myself that it won't be long before they have Mickey Mouse and Donald Duck on the evening news.

On a deeper level, of course, it's no laughing matter. When the power of the press is exercised in concert with the political machinery that is in place today—I'm talking about the right-wing shift in American politics—what you have is a dangerous, malevolent concoction. It might sound paranoid, but that's what you have.

Just recently there's been considerable controversy about the planes that were shot down over Cuba. The alternative press is asking some interesting questions, but what about the mainstream media? There's a whole history to this incident that is being withheld by the government and the press. I can't help wondering about the fact that when Cuba was the whorehouse of the Caribbean—when it was a Mafia safe-haven—you didn't hear anybody talking about invading Cuba or changing the government. It was only when a government of the Cubans' own choice rose to power and said that they were no longer willing to be our whorehouse—"We are an independent sovereign country, and we will have the government we want, not the government you want"—that our government began plotting to kill President Castro and to destroy Cuba through an economic blockade that, according to inter-national law, amounted to an act of war. Has our government, our press, acted on the right side of history? Have they stood on the right side of fun-damental justice?

Cuba's only one of many examples. Fundamental-ly, the United States government has allied itself for decades with some of the darkest forces in history for the sake of economic gain, for politi-cal self-interest, for the protection of the status quo. And it continues to do so, domestically as well. That's why we have the likes of David Duke running for governor and the likes of Pat Buchanan running for president (in spite of having Klansmen on his staff). It's why everybody is talking about welfare queens and slamming the poor. It is also why the safest political platform of the decade is based on promises of "getting tough on crime." Their line is that it's okay to despise the poor, because they have it "too good" anyway. Besides, they claim, it's the poor, the minorities who are causing a rise in violent crime: "What we need is more executions. What we need to do is start chop-ping people's heads off. . . ." The level of political discourse in our country is anti-life. And the press is not innocent.

Violence

Yet that's exactly what the system believes in, what the system preaches, what the system practices: violence. Certainly I believe in the necessity of fighting the system, and in the necessity of self-defense, but I'm *not* going to employ the same tactics and methods the system uses every day. Why replace the system with the same thing?

We need a *new* system, one where people are free of the violence of the system. I may not be a pacifist, but I still hope for a day when there are no bombs, no guns—no weapons whatsoever—no war, poverty, or other injustices; no social and class hatreds; no crime and no prisons.

I reject the tools and weapons of violence.

God-talk

Then Almitra spoke, saying, We would ask now of Death.

And he said:

You would know the secret of death.

But how shall you find it unless you seek it in the heart of life?

The owl whose night-bound eyes are blind unto the day cannot unveil the mystery of light.

If you would indeed behold the spirit of death, open your heart wide unto the body of life.

For life and death are one, even as river and the sea are one.

Kahlil Gibran, *The Prophet*

ON DEATH'S BRINK, men begin to see things they've perhaps never seen before. Like those around them, and especially those who share their fate. Men on Phase II—men whose death warrants have been signed, men with a date to die—live each day with a clarity and vibrancy they might have lacked in less pressured times. In the state's icebox, behind the clear plastic shield that separates death row proper from Phase II, sounds from the six death warrant cells are muffled from the rest of the block.

Men on the "Faze" spend their precious hours doing whatever concerns them most, and for many that means talking and learning about each other, their depths, their heights, their human uniqueness.

It is midnight, the end of a long, humid July day, yet conversation continues in earnest:

"You ever think of outer space?"
"Hell, yeah!"
"Really?"
"Yeah, man—alla time."
"No shit? Like what kinda stuff?"
"All kindsa stuff—like the vastness of space, black holes, how impossible a lotta that stuff they show on sci-fi movies is; inner space . . . a lotta stuff, Scott."
"Humph. Well, tell me summa the stuff you be thinkin' of, Mu—break down what you mean."
"Well, you know how in alla *Star Wars*– and *Star Trek*–type joints, when a ship gets hit, you hear these huge KA-BOOM! explosions, and see fireballs and shit?"
"Uh-huh."
"That's impossible."
"Why you say that?"

"Coz. Dig—in space, there's a vacuum—no oxygen
—so how can sound travel? To the extent there'd
be an explosion, it would be silent."
"OK. What other stuff?"
"Well, you know how dudes ina movie talk about
lightspeed, 'warp factor seven,' and all that?"
"Uh-huh."
"Dig this, Scott. The smallest subatomic particle in
light is the photon; that's what's movin' atta speed
of light, and it moves so quickly 'coz it got no
mass. Once you add mass, a ship, provisions, human bodies, you slow everything down—so all that
warp seven, faster-than-light stuff is impossible."
"Damn, Mu—how'd you get into that shit?"
"I read. Science. Einstein. Stephen Hawking. Science
fiction. Asimov. Herbert. Bisson—alla them dudes."
"No shit, Mu! All right. Here's one for ya: What,
or who is God? Whoa! Do you believe in God?"
"Absolutely."
"Well?"
"Each man, based on his own understanding,
creates his own gods. Every person in creation
has his own idea of God. Now, are they all wrong?
Yes—and no. "Everybody worships somethin'. They
might not give it the name 'God,' but what they
spend their time, their minds, their consciousness
on—that's their God. It might be money; drugs;
sex. The communists in Russia wouldn't say it
in those words, but Marx and Lenin were gods

to them, even though they claimed to renounce religion.

"God is divine intelligence. God is life. God is the force that keeps this creation in existence."

"But *who* is God? What's his name?" "Why *his?*"

"What you mean, man?"

"I mean—dig this . . . . There's hundreds of names for God, right?"

"Yup—"

"Man gave God these names, based on culture, history, their own perceptions—so, how dya think 'God' got sex—a God that created both sexes?"

"You sayin' God's a female?"

"Naw, man—I ain't saying God is a woman; I'm saying God is beyond man or woman—beyond sex, and therefore as much mother, if not more so, as father."

"How can you say that, man? You just said 'beyond woman.' How can God be beyond woman, and also mother?"

"Well—I mean, in terms of function. Dig this. In all cultures, among almost all of nature, the mother is she who truly cares, who feeds, cleans, hugs—y' know?—for all her children. Think of mother earth: all that we know, that we see, that we eat, that we wear, comes from mother earth. Man might combine things, mix things up, but he don't create nothin'. Mama—God—creates or brings into creation all that is. Think of it this way, Scott . . . ."

"I'm wicha, Mu . . . ."

"Of all the planets in this entire solar system: why is Earth just right for us? Mars and Venus? Too hot. Jupiter? Too gaseous. Pluto? Too cold. This Earth is *just* right! That ain't no coincidence, man."

"Hey, man. I was just checkin' you out. I've often thought those exact, same things—I didn't know *you* wuz into that, man—I had no idea!"

"Why not?"

"Well, I knew you was into nature—but this stuff?"

"Hey—ain't God 'natural'? Ain't Earth? Ain't all of creation—all that is?"

"I know that, man—but—hey! I'm surprised!"

"Well, to be perfectly honest, I'm surprised too!"

"Yeah? Now don't go off on me, but . . ."

"I ain't—why?"

"Well, I thought you wuza bona fide *nut!*" Scott erupts ina fit of laughter—

"I'm serious, man."

His laughter continues . . . .

"See, down Huntington, guys said you wuza secret squirrel-type dude—talkin' 'bout spies 'n' shit, real crazy stuff . . . . When you told me 'bout gov'ment files, I looked to my own experience. Y'know, the gov'ment bugged me for years and years, when I was in my young teens . . . ."

"Oh yeah?"

"Yup—If I told dudes about it, they'd be whisperin'

the same stuff 'bout me—'that nigga's crazy; he into some secret squirrel-type shit . . . . ' Y'know the rap."

"Yeah, I do."

"Coz they don't know—unless they hadda experience."

"That's it! Now, let's get into black holes—you into that?"

"Well, I read some stuff 'bout it."

"Do you think a human could survive in it?"

"Nope."

"Why not?"

"Well . . . ."

The men talk on—hour after hour, late into the night, early into morn. Days, hours away from a date with death, they finally see each other.

They see the miracles of life, the miracle of each other.

Lawd, Lawd, I look at you and see
    a man on a cross who don't look like me.
I wonder if you can truly be
God of all eternity—
maker of earth, the wind, the sea,
maker, even, of lil' old black me?

Meditations on the Cross

by Rufus, a slave

Lawd, Lawd, I look at the cross and pray—
Can you hear the words I say?
Can you see the things I do?
Things done by folks
    who look like you?
Can you snap these chains offa my feet?
Can you make it so's I don't get beat?
Can you bring my wife,
    son, daughter back to me?
Can you bring an end to slavery?
Lawd, O Lawd—can you truly make us free?

Come to think of it, why am I
    asking you?
What I mean to say is—
    what can you do?
Your hands is nailed to this here cross—
How could you ever be the Big Boss?

Also nailed is your two feets—
    you cain't even walk the streets!
And on your head, that crown
    of thorns,
Will it stop new ideas
    from being born?

Lawd, I don't mean to sound too smart,
    it's just that these things be in my heart;
The last time I thought of you,
    was when they lynched my daddy, Lou—
They tied his hands and bound his feet,
    lashed him, slashed him like a piece of meat,
    cut him, burned him, and just before they let him die,
    they hung him from a tree, swingin' high.
How could your people do this, Lawd?
How could you give them the Power of the sword?
How could you let 'em hang Daddy on a tree,
    when that's the very same thing they did to thee?
How could you let 'em bring us here as slaves
    over roiling miles of ocean waves?
How could you do this, Jesus,
Weren't you king of the Jews—
Weren't they themselves broken and beaten,
    battered and abused?

Lawd, O Lawd, I ain't tryin' to be
    no big man,
I'm just tryin' to understand.
And if you don't wanna speak to me,
    can't you at least let me see?
Ol' preacher say you died for the poor;
Does that mean we won't be poor no more?
I'm not try'na run things in heaven above,
I just wan' freedom, my family, Love.
They say it's compassion
    your life demonstrated,
but I wonder, if that's so,
    why am I hated?

Well, Lawd, I guess I gotta go,
It's just that I'd like to be more in the know.
Just think of this as my personal letter,
    asking how things could be made better—
Finally, Lawd, lemme say I Love You,
    'cause you went through the same
    hell as we still do.

Holiday Thoughts

IN EACH YEAR'S wintry season comes the great festival in the West alleged to celebrate the birth of Jesus of Nazareth some two thousand years ago. To many, however, it is a time of utter hypocrisy. To those many millions mired in poverty, it is a time of bitter cold, a time of no respite from the hours spent huddled in windswept alleys. It is, they say, "the season to be jolly," but for far too many it is a season of need, an hour of aching loneliness.

The faceless millions sing of cheer and charity, but I, who sit among the hopeless and the living dead, among those who populate your prisons and dungeons of death, see neither cheer nor charity, but rather falseness, gaudiness, and empty flash. The only things not empty are the tills of the merchants, because for most, Christmas is celebrated not in remembrance of the Christ, but to fill the coffers. Who remembers that the carols are sung in praise of a prisoner, indeed, a death row prisoner destined to face crucifixion? What mean cheer and charity to those who face more modern methods of execution?

John Africa

> . . . You judges are confusing God's right of
> self-defense with *your* way of legal destruction
> because you are confused about the meaning of
> right, the purpose of defense, the existence of true
> freedom, the law of God. A person's defense is a
> God-given power that must not be tampered with;
> this is *God's* law . . .
>
> John Africa, *The Judges' Letter*

UNTRAINED, UNTAUGHT, AND UNTAMED, John Africa
attracted a wide range of people to a small room in
West Philadelphia; men and women who had one thing
in common: need. Their needs were as various as were
their personalities. Some sought a respite from the social storms that raged across America in the late 1960s;
some, answers to the Great Questions that plagued
their minds; others sought the healing of denatured,
weakened bodies; still others the security of a family to
replace their shattered birth families. In a sense, all of
them sought that most illusive of quarries—Truth.

All found their various needs addressed, answered, and
met in one way or another by this most remarkable of
men. For John Africa was a man blessed with shimmering wisdom, enormous patience, and powerful passions.

He did what healers do: he healed. He did what
teachers do: he taught. He did what carpenters do:
he built. Using neither nails nor lumber, he constructed from the fabric of the heart a tightly knit,
cohesive body of brothers and sisters called MOVE.[1]

Bold beyond belief, and so fearless they seemed
reckless, these men and women burned with the
zeal of a new, rebellious faith, and spread the
revolutionary teaching of John Africa far and wide.
Living as they did in a land of unfreedom—in a city
whose past may well be marked by a legacy of free
thought, but whose present stands on the legs
of repression—it was only natural that they were
labeled public enemies even as they fought for freedom. It was predictable that their path should take
them into the eye of the storm.

Yet nothing could stop them as they confronted
and battled the forces of the state: not broken
bones, not police bullets, not jail cells, not government bombs. Not even death—witness the urban
holocaust of May 13, 1985, when Philadelphia
police and federal government agents massacred
eleven MOVE men, women, and children. Despite
this premeditated mass murder, MOVE is still alive
and well, still spreading its teaching—and still doing what its founder-carpenter did: building.

Bombs have not stopped them. Nine hundred years

1. Not an acronym, the name MOVE simply expresses it members'
belief that life is movement; that all things exist "on a move."

in cages have not stopped them.[2] Repeated acts of police-sponsored terrorism have not intimidated them. After such remarkable resilience, the question must be asked, "How?" Who united this disparate group of people; what inspired these ordinary folks to feats of extraordinary commitment in the face of the most repressive government assaults in contemporary history? The answer can only be, "John Africa." Consider his words:

> . . . It is past time for all poor people to release themselves from the deceptive strangulation of society, realize that society has failed you; for to attempt to ignore this system of deception *now* is to deny you the need to protest this failure *later*. The system has failed you yesterday, failed you today, and has created the conditions for failure tomorrow. . . .

The brave and beautiful men and women of MOVE took these words and translated them into action. They knew them to contain power, wisdom, and a shattering truth.

---

2. On August 8, 1978, after a brutal police assault on MOVE during which their home in the Powelton Village section of West Philadelphia was destroyed, nine members of the organization were arrested for allegedly killing James Ramp, a police officer. These "suspects" were in the basement of their home at the time of the shooting; Ramp, who was facing the house on the street above them, was shot from the back. Several MOVE sympathizers were arrested too but released after agreeing to renounce their ties to MOVE. Convicted and sentenced (30–100 years each) in a trial marked by blatant racial and political bias, the "MOVE 9" remain incarcerated in Pennsylvania prisons. They, and growing numbers of supporters across the country, continue to maintain their innocence.

U N T I T L E D

What power governs the stars above,
Which makes them be,
Which pours the sea,
Which stirs the cup of eternity?
What can this force be—but Love?

Why fight over a name?
For who can win this deadly game?
Why battle over religion,
When we stand on the brink of perdition?

Who rolls the dice?
Who grows the rice?
Who brings us into being twice.
Made earth and water, fire and ice?

Who plants the seed of the flower of life,
Creates and carves with a living knife,
Brings oneness by joining husband and wife
'Mid human turmoil, hatred, strife?
What can this force be—but Love?

The very development of American society is creating a new kind of blindness about poverty. The poor are increasingly slipping out of the very experience and consciousness of the nation.

Michael Harrington, *The Other America*

MORE WAR FOR THE POOR

IN A MOVE THAT was as chilling as it was Malthusian, President Bill "Bubba" Clinton signed a so-called welfare "reform" (read "destruction") bill that neither Reagan nor Bush, even in their finest hours, could have succeeded in passing.

In this one act, by affixing his name to this legislative obscenity, the Man from Hope dashed the hopes of millions of the poor, all in order to protect his political ass.

In this age of triumphant capitalism, "poor" has become synonymous with "bad," which is rather ironic for a president who trumpeted his own poor Arkansan origins, though carefully restyling them as New Age Lincolnesque.

Masked by promises of "helping the poor" and emboldened by the *Bruderbund* of fellow Republicans, the Democrats have sacrificed poor men, women, and children upon the fiery brazier of political ambition.

In Frazer's classic *The Golden Bough* (1890), the Scottish anthropologist and classicist describes an ancient sacrifice:

> When the Carthaginians were defeated and besieged by Agathocles, they ascribed their disasters to the wrath of Baal; for whereas in former times they had been wont to sacrifice to him their own children, they had latterly fallen into the habit of buying children and rearing them to be victims. So, to appease the angry god, two hundred children of the noblest families were picked out for sacrifice. . . . They were sacrificed by being placed, one by one, on the sloping hands of the brazen image, from which they rolled into a pit of fire. . . . (236)

Let me tell you: *that* was a nobler sacrifice than is this! For the sacrifice of those in antiquity occurred under the belief—albeit a misapprehension—that such an act would allay worse chaos from a vengeful god.

Why are the poor among us today to be sacrificed? To satisfy a mere misapprehension? To balance a national budget? Hardly. Less than two percent of the nation's budget pays for welfare, so it is not likely to bust under its weight. Then why?

In the past, whenever reports of higher employment levels surfaced, the news sent Wall Street into a panicked fall. Good news to most of us, it caused a sea of frowns on financial markets. It is these very markets, the power centers of capital, that dictate the actions of politicians, including their abolition of social safety nets such as welfare.

When millions starve, workers duly fall to silent acquiescence for fear of losing what little they have. Fear creates a cowed labor force which, when faced with givebacks, won't even whimper. High poverty signals capitalism triumphant.

Of Becoming

RECENTLY I WAS asked to send a statement for a youth conference, something that would be read at an opening gathering or something. When I thought about it, a question arose in my mind. This is the question: What is the difference between an oak tree and an acorn? I've been thinking of this as I think of you—of young people from various paths of life converging in search of what is real, what is whole, and what is worthy of your time and attention.

At first, the differences between a mighty oak and the tiny green acorn seem humongous. But upon reflection, one sees that the only real difference between them is time. You are living acorns in the forest of life, with all the potential, all the powers of the most massive oak tree that ever grew. You are, in your seeking, in the process of becoming.

In my memory, at least, youth is a most difficult time.

It is a time of emotions, of tossing and turning, of grappling with questions that bore to the very heart of existence, and with the unsatisfactory answers often given in return.

But this is *your* time—your time to delve, to dig, to plow the rich, fertile earth of yourselves. There you will find every answer worth giving. You are at that place in time when you have learned one of the most powerful truths: that sometimes we older folks just don't have the answers.

I therefore urge you to dig on, until the treasure of truth is unearthed in each of you, and once gained, is brought to life. Your task is not easy, but it is necessary. For tomorrow's forests must be treed by you.

ANOTHER THING that comes to mind: you young adults should recognize that however you look at it, you will never again be as free as you are now, in this phase of life. Marriage, for example, poses obligations, and so does a career. So if you have the opportunity to study, to row in the life of the mind, use it. You are at a level of freedom you may not and probably will not experience for decades. Feed your mind, not just with information, but with knowledge that feeds your deeper, inner self. Ask questions about what you see, hear, and read— also of yourselves.

Again, this is the freedom phase of your life. Do
not underestimate the worth and the wealth of
this phase. Now is the time you can best move to
change the world. And worlds can change, even
if the change starts only in your mind, in your
perception.

A Call to Action

The choice, as every choice, is yours:

to fight for freedom or be fettered,

to struggle for liberty or be satisfied with slavery,

to side with life or death.

Spread the word of life far and wide.

Talk to your friends, read, and open your eyes—

even to doorways of perception you feared

to look into yesterday.

Hold your heart open to the truth.

INTERVIEW WITH MUMIA

Allen Hougland

Pennsylvania's new "control unit" prison, the State Correctional Institution at Waynesburg (SCI Greene), hides in rural hills just fifteen miles from the West Virginia border. Its low earth-toned block walls blend into the grassy clearing where it furtively crouches, surrounded by multiple layers of green metal fences ringed with double-edged razor wire.

Once inside, video producer Thomas Filmyer and I follow a genial female administrator through the stark bright corridors, passing through a series of sliding metal security doors to a cubicle where we will spend 90 minutes with Mumia Abu-Jamal.

As we enter the little cinderblock room, the official places herself outside; the door remains open during the interview. Mumia is already seated, wearing a blue cotton shirt and steel handcuffs, long dreadlocks hanging over his shoulders. Appearing healthy and relaxed, he seems eager to begin talking. His deep voice echoes as it filters through narrow strips of screen at the ends of the thick Plexiglas barrier that separates him from us.

AH: Can you tell us who you are, in your own words?

MAJ: My name is Mumia Abu-Jamal, I'm in my early forties. I've been on death row since July of 1982—

in fact, I've been on several death rows in Pennsylvania, in the United States of America. Despite my
penal status I'm a writer, a journalist, a columnist,
and a professional revolutionary.

AH: And you grew up in Philadelphia?

MAJ: I spent much of my youth in Philadelphia. As
part of my membership in the Black Panther Party,
I also spent time in other cities, working in other
chapters of that organization. The bulk of my most
formative years were spent in North Philly, in the
heart of North Philadelphia.

AH: How would you describe your childhood there?

MAJ: Average—absolutely unremarkable. Except,
one would have to admit, for my exposure to the
Black Panther Party, there's nothing remarkable
about my childhood that distinguishes me from
millions of other young kids of my generation. I
grew up in a poor neighborhood, in what's com-
monly called the "peejays" or the projects, and
spent most of my educational years in Philadelphia,
in elementary schools, junior high schools, and
high schools. What makes it really unremarkable is
the context of the times we're talking about—the
late 1960s and early 1970s, which was the explosion era of the black liberation movement. So there
were many people of my generation who were
active in the Black Panther Party, the Republic of
New Africa, the Southern Nonviolent Coordinating

Committee, the Nation of Islam, and other organizations that were overtly active at that time.

AH: You were born with a different name—not Mumia Abu-Jamal, but Wesley Cook, right?

MAJ: Yes.

AH: When and why did you change your name?

MAJ: It was a change that took place over a transition of years—not one day it was one name, and another day the next. Again, in the context of the times, in the years when the black liberation movement was growing and attracting the adherence of people who believed in that movement, many of us took African names. One of my teachers in a black high school in Philadelphia was actually a Kenyan who had come to teach Swahili. And it was his practice in his Swahili class to give names to students that were African. So that was my name: Mumia.

AH: And then the Abu-Jamal?

MAJ: Well, I'm actually named after my first son. It means "father of Jamal," and my first son is named Jamal. It's kind of a mix, in that my first name is Swahili, and my middle and last names are Arabic.

AH: How did your involvement with the Panthers go, and how did it not go, and how did it come to an end?

MAJ: I remember—and of course we're talking about decades ago now—but I remember it was probably one of the most exciting and liberational times of my life. Of course, for most people, their teen years are a time of freedom. Mine were a time of ultra, super freedom. It was a tremendous learning experience. The very fact that I, even from this place, am a journalist who writes and communicates with thousands and thousands of people every week—its embryo can be found in the fact that I worked as a Panther in what's called the Ministry of Information. That means I worked filing reports to the national Black Panther Party journal called *Black Panther—Black Community News Service* based in San Francisco and Oakland, California. But we also had regional papers that came out, like throwaways or giveaways. I worked for the Ministry of Information in Philadelphia, in New York, and in other cities. So I was trained as a revolutionary journalist, trained to present the positions of the Black Panther Party from that revolutionary—black revolutionary—perspective.

I should add that many times, people will talk about that experience of mine, not from a position of knowledge, but from a position of opinion, and say, "well, that wasn't 'mainstream' journalism" or "when did you get into 'mainstream' journalism?" Of course, I hold that that experience *was* one of mainstream journalism. What does mainstream

journalism mean if it does not mean that someone writes, edits, does graphic arts—because
in the Party we learned to do everything—for a
newspaper that is read by over 250,000 people
a week? How many papers have a circulation that
expansive? It was an international circulation. We
covered international news, we *made* international
news. Because at one point, at the Party's highest
point—before COINTELPRO ripped it asunder—
came the establishment of the Party's international
office in North Africa, in Algiers. It was called the
Inter-communal Section, under the former Minister of Information, Eldridge Cleaver. In essence,
it was African-America's first international embassy—an independent embassy of revolutionary
African-America, where people all over the world
could come and talk without the intercession of
the United States government.

And I say "without the intercession of the United
States government" because it is only fair, it is
only honest, it is only accurate to point out that
the function of the United States government
at that time, and before and since, has been to
retard, destroy, disrupt, and tear asunder the black
liberation and black nationalist movements of that
period. That's proven by FBI files that have been
released after the fact. How many people who
celebrate the memory of the birthday of Dr. Martin
Luther King, Jr. know that the FBI hounded him

relentlessly, tapped his phones and hotel rooms, worked through snitches, with the full blessings of the United States Government at the highest levels—I mean in the White House? How many people know that's true of A. Philip Randolph, the African-American labor leader who helped create the march on Washington back in the early 1960s? Or Marcus Garvey? Or Malcolm X? The list can go on and on. There's also Adam Clayton Powell, who was a Congressman from Harlem. Here he was, a Congressman, and he was under complete and total surveillance by the government of which he was a member. The late J. Edgar Hoover made it very clear that the function of the FBI was to prevent the rise of a black messiah: anyone who could unite black America into one cohesive force.

AH: Where did he say that?

MAJ: He said that in his COINTELPRO papers, in his files. That's in the FBI files. If anyone finds that what I'm saying is in the least incredible, I would invite them to read a book written by a professor of political science named Kenneth O'Reilly. The book is called *Black Americans: The FBI Files* [Carroll & Graf, 1994].

AH: And so you felt the need for black revolution?

MAJ: Absolutely.

AH: What do you mean by that exactly, when you say "black revolution?"

MAJ: The word revolution means transformation; it means change. When one considers from any objective perspective the condition of African-American people in this country—if you didn't find the need to change that condition for the better, then your interest was to keep things as they were, to preserve the status quo. If you look at the condition of African-Americans today, we're at the bottom of every social indicator—in terms of educational attainment, in terms of work income, in terms of our life expectancy, in terms of our health. Every indicator of social well-being and status. Why are we at the bottom of those lists? I would say that it isn't a reality that could be isolated in 1970. It is a reality that continues to this day. Revolution is a necessity. Change is necessary—to change a situation that is deadly to us.

AH: I have two quotes I want to read you. One of them from Frederick Douglass, saying: "Power concedes nothing without a demand." And the other, which you are quoted as having once said: "Political power grows out of the barrel of a gun." I'd like you to talk about those two statements.

MAJ: Frederick Douglass may have said that over a hundred and fifty years ago, but that truth is certainly evident today, and will be evident for as long as men live. "Power concedes nothing without a demand." To the extent that African-Americans have moved out of *de facto* segregation and slavery in this country—that didn't happen because one day America woke up and said, "I think we should give African-Americans their voting rights; we should stop discrimination against them in jobs and housing and so forth." No, it didn't happen like that. It happened because of the actions, the strategies, and the pains and the deaths, finally, of people like Dr. Martin Luther King, like Malcolm X, like Dr. Huey P. Newton—people from a wide range of philosophical and ideological positions, people who made those demands on power. Had there not been a Malcolm X, there would not have been the effectiveness of a Dr. Martin Luther King, because both of them, in their different roles, communicated to the power structure: "We'd better go this way, or this way there'll be a consequence."

To the latter quotation, which—I should say—is from Chairman Mao Zedong of the Chinese Communist Party—that was something that was used in my case, as a justification to give me the death penalty. In the case *Dawson v. Delaware,* in which the prosecutor introduced the defendant's Aryan Brotherhood membership, the U.S. Supreme Court found that violated his First Amendment right of association. Well, in the penalty phase of my trial, the prosecution introduced my membership of over a decade before, as a teenager, in the Black Panther Party. To a predominantly white jury, some of whom were relatives of police officers—come on! What about the membership of the judge in the Fraternal Order of Police? That's irrelevant? When we raised that, he said "Well, I was only a member for a few years." Well damn, I was only a member of the Black Panther Party for a few years. There's not even the appearance of balance here.

Thomas Filmyer/WCB

I think it only fair at this point to respond to the quote as I did then, when it was raised: how did Americans (or people who call themselves Americans) —how did they acquire political power here in this country, if not through a gun? How did they prevail over the forces of the Crown, of Britain, in the so-called Revolutionary War, if not through the power and force of arms? How did they prevail over the native peoples of this country in the so-called Indian Wars, if not through force of arms? So one does not have to say this is a communist sentiment or a radical sentiment. It is a sentiment that arises from history, and is undeniable. It's very curious how people will talk about how proud they are to be an American, and ignore the very roots of what being American came from. If Americans did not fight with all the tools at their command—including guns—against the British, we'd all be speaking with a British accent and saying "God save the Queen."

AH: Mumia, about your later journalism work. Your work was guided by, you said, "the principle that we are oppressed black human beings first." As a result of the work you did in Philadelphia and in the U.S. in general in the 1970s, you became known as "the voice of the voiceless," especially as regards the group MOVE. Can you talk about your later journalism work, and also tell us who MOVE is?

MAJ: Sure, that would be my honor. MOVE is a family of revolutionaries, of naturalist revolutionaries, founded in Philadelphia in the late 1960s/early 1970s, who oppose all that this system represents. For years in Philadelphia, there's been continual and unrelenting conflict between the MOVE organization and the city—that is, the police, the judiciary, and the political arm of the system. They have fought it bitterly. We reporters have a herd mentality. Reporters tend to do what other reporters do—it's almost like herd instinct. The "herd" in Philadelphia was describing MOVE in frankly animalistic or subhuman terms. I remember an editorial that appeared in the *Philadelphia Inquirer* that used, I think, precisely those terms: it said they were "subhuman." Wow! That was an editorial that just expressed a tone that was reflected in the coverage. Based on what I had read in the newspapers, I could not say that MOVE were my favorite people—probably the opposite was the truth.

But I found something out that was very interesting when I began covering MOVE as part of my work as a reporter for a radio station that's now known as WWDB, WHAT at that time: I found out they were human beings. That doesn't sound like an earth-shattering revelation now, but it was then, because the complete dehumanization of them was almost total in terms of how local and regional media projected this group—as though they were literally beyond the pale. What I found were idealistic, committed, strong, unshakable men and women who had a deep spirit-level aversion to everything this system represents. To them, this system was a death system involved in a deathly war. To them, everything this system radiated was poison—from its technological waste to its destruction of the earth, to its destruction of the air and water, to its destruction of the very genetic pool of human life and animal life and all life. MOVE opposed all this bitterly and unrelentingly, without compromise.

I remember the first time I heard about MOVE— perhaps it was a television report—in the early seventies. Some of the MOVE people had gotten busted, and the gist of the television broadcast was: "These nuts, these crazy people, were protest- ing outside the zoo for no reason." Of course they didn't explain what MOVE's position was. Well, what you found later, when you got closer and began examining the reality, was that according to the teachings of MOVE's founder, John Africa, all life—*all* life—is sacred and has worth, and should not be exploited for money and profit. MOVE people were busted because they were protesting the reality of the zoo, which they called a "prison" for animal life. Today you have groups like Earth First and so forth, across the world, who embrace many of those same positions that were once called bizarre. MOVE did it twenty years ago. What I found was a remarkable and incredible family that continues to thrive, to grow, to grow stronger, to build, and to touch bases with people. I mean, if someone told me twenty years ago that there would be MOVE support groups in London and Paris, I'd have said: "Get out of here, you're out of your mind!" Today that's a reality.

AH: Do you consider MOVE founder John Africa to be your spiritual leader?

MAJ: Yes, absolutely, without question.

AH: When you talk about faith, your faith—because you do bring up faith—what do you mean?

MAJ: Faith simply means belief. People can put all kinds of tags and clothing on it and call it whatever they want to call it. But what you believe in, what has resonance for you, in your deepest self—that's truly your faith. To some people that's money. To many, I guess, millions in America—they will talk about "In God We Trust," but guess what—they really trust money. Their faith, their real self, revolves around currency, money, wealth, status—those kinds of things. I found in the teachings of John Africa a truth that was undeniable, that was powerful, that was naked, that was raw. And it talked about this system in a way that I wish I had the guts to talk about it and I wish I had the clarity to talk about it. MOVE members talked about it uncompromisingly, and not just talked about it, but lived it every day. In America we talk about religion. If you're Christian, you talk about Sunday. That's your religion: Sunday you go to church, Monday you do your thing. And the next Sunday you go back to church, and the next Monday you do your thing again. If you're Jewish, then Saturday is your Sabbath, and you go to temple and you say your prayers. If you're Muslim, then Friday is your day *Juma'at.* And what all of these religions really suggest in these days and times is a kind of compartmentalization of faith—"this is your holy day." To MOVE, all days are holy days, because all life is holy. When you're out fighting for your brothers and sisters, you're practicing your religion. Faith means what you truly, absolutely believe. If you ask a MOVE person, "What is your religion?" he'll say "life."

AH: What would you say to the critics of MOVE and to people in the neighborhoods where they lived who have said that they were a disruption, a nuisance; that they were dirty, that they were noisy, that they were constantly proselytizing to the neighborhood and violating their neighbors' right to live in peace?

MAJ: I would say this—and assume for the sake of argument that all of those criticisms were absolutely true: How noisy is a bomb? How disruptive is the destruction of sixty-one houses by fire? How alienating is massacre and mass murder? Because that's what the city gave people who said: "These MOVE nuts are a pain in our ass."

AH: Of course we're talking about the bombing of the MOVE house on Osage Avenue in Philadelphia in 1985.

MAJ: Yes. On May 13, 1985, the city of Philadelphia literally shot tens of thousands of rounds into that house on Osage Avenue, and dropped a bomb, and let the fire burn for ten or twelve hours. And it consumed sixty-one houses, at last count. Was that disruptive of their neighborhood rights? Was that disruptive of life itself? Was that disturbing? I think that many people found themselves suckered by a political and police system that used neighborhood conflict and intensified it into urban war and almost Armageddon. I've lived in several parts of that city and in other cities. I've had neighbors who were pains in the ass—I've had people play their music, and no matter what you said, you couldn't get them to turn it down, not unless you wanted to go down there and get into a fistfight or something. In many neighborhoods, in Southwest Philadelphia today, you can't stick your head out the door without hearing submachine gun fire. Is that disruptive? Is the neighborhood alarmed when some drug-addicted punk pulls out an Uzi and shoots at a competitor? You got crack dealing, you got prostitution —you have all the ills of society. But you know what you don't have? You don't have the government come down as if in a war as they did on May 13, 1985. You don't have that. Unless you have MOVE rebels and revolutionaries in their homes. . . .

AH: Mumia, about the death penalty—with which you're well acquainted—you have said that, "where the death penalty is concerned, law follows politics." And we have seen a change, an evolution—if you want to call it that—in death penalty law over the last twenty or twenty-five years.

MAJ: It might best be called a "devolution."

AH: Yes—from the U.S. Supreme Court case *Furman v. Georgia,* which declared the death penalty unconstitutional as it was being applied at that time, 1972; through *Gregg v. Georgia* in 1976, which declared the death penalty would be con-

Thomas Filmyer/WCB

stitutional
if "guided
discretion"
were used in
sentencing,
requiring
"objective
standards" to
be followed.
Since then
there has
been a new
tide of capital
punishment
in this coun-
try, with over three thousand condemned now.
And the current Supreme Court seems inclined to
curb the rights of appeal of the condemned. This
is happening at the same time that other industri-
alized nations have all backed away from capital
punishment. Can you talk about why you think it
is that this country has devoted itself so whole-
heartedly to executions at this point in time?

MAJ: I think the impetus for that reality arises from
the same source from which arises the impetus
for the unprecedented levels of incarceration of
African-Americans, as compared with other sectors
of the American population. I don't think it's a
coincidence that this is happening in the United

States of America. If you look at another North
American society that is very, very similar in its
history, you find a completely different reality. The
society I'm speaking of, of course, is Canada. We
share the same temporal space, the same conti-
nent, for the most part (except for Quebec) the
same language, the same general Anglo-oriented
legal traditions. Yet there you find no capital punishment. There you find a completely different perspective when one talks about the penal system—
the so-called correctional system. There it's almost
unheard of for a man to be sentenced to more
than twenty years in prison—it has to be a mass
ax-murder type of situation. And when you look
at Canada and you examine it, and you look at the
United States and you examine it, the elements
that differ between those two societies cohere, I
think, around the issue of race, around the issue of
this country's history as a slave society, who rele-
gated an entire people to a sub-human status.

In the infamous *Dred Scott* opinion of 1857, U.S.
Chief Justice Roger Brooks Taney said: "A Negro
has no rights that a white man is bound to respect." In that seminal case, the Supreme Court denied a petition of a slave for his freedom. He said:
"I live in a free state, where there is no slavery, and
therefore my slave status should be invalidated as
a matter of law." The overwhelming majority of the
United States Supreme Court, of Justice Taney's

court said: "Uh-uh, you're wrong." What they said
was:

> When the Constitution and the Declaration
> of Independence were written, Africans were
> perceived as three-fifths of a person. When
> one speaks of "we the people," we were
> certainly not speaking of you. And there-
> fore we cannot now give you the rights and
> appurtenances that apply to "we the people."
> The Constitution has no relevance to you and
> your kind, or to your descendants should
> they ever become free.

That's in the words of the *Dred Scott* opinion.
And that spirit continues to resonate throughout
American law.

People who are sticklers would say: "Well, the
Fourteenth Amendment surely overruled that
case." But if you look at that case and you examine its precedent, you will find that to this day,
that case has yet to be *judicially* overruled. And
where humans actually come in contact with their
government is not in the voting booth—I mean,
that's an empty formality for many—but it's in the
courtroom. That's where most people literally meet
their government. And it's in that courtroom where
people find whether the rights they're told about
truly exist, or don't exist. And for all intents and
purposes, if one is poor, if one is African-American,

if one lacks influence and power, then you come into that courtroom without the hope that you will walk out a free man. That is the undeniable reality in America.

The death penalty is unique in American law, in that if you really examine the process, you'll come away with a lot of curious ideas about how it works in reality, as opposed to how it's supposed to work in theory. I'll tell you why. In capital case law, unlike any other law, from the very beginning, under the case *Wainright v. Witt,* a juror can be excluded if he or she has any opinion against capital punishment. So therefore you have what's called a proprosecution jury—from the beginning—who must swear that they can give the death penalty before they hear one word of evidence. Studies have shown this jury is prone to convict, that it is pro-prosecution and anti-defendant in the extreme, compared to any other jury in American jurisprudence. That's how you begin the process.

Isn't it also odd that at this stage of the process, where you're under the threat of having not just your liberty but your life stolen by the state, you're equipped with the worst counsel the system provides—court-appointed counsel, with no financial resources. Often, while they may have good hearts, they have the least training, because capital case law is distinct from any other kind of law. In Philadelphia, if a person is charged with a capital offense, he gets a court appointed lawyer. At the time of my trial, the fee for the lawyer was only $2,500. Out of that, he was supposed to provide investigators, ballisticians, forensic experts, psychologists, whatever. He was a sole practitioner—he had no investigator, no paralegal—he had a secretary and himself. We had absolutely no resources. We had nothing. I didn't have to be a wild-eyed, raving, Black Panther or MOVE maniac to say: "Fuck, I'll represent myself." If all he could do was get a motion denied, I could do that. But the court denied me my constitutional right to represent myself. They insisted this guy take over my defense, first as backup counsel and later as lead counsel. I didn't want him as lead counsel—or backup counsel, for that matter.

AH: Do you think he really cared?

MAJ: I think that he cared at the beginning, but our relationship as client and counsel really deteriorated—when he was put in the position of backup counsel, all that went out the window. Because he testified under oath that for four or five weeks he sat on his hands. He later got up at a hearing and said: "I was ineffective." And the district attorney said: "No, you weren't ineffective. You were a great lawyer—it was just that your client was really difficult, right?" And he said: "No, I was ineffective. I didn't do what I should have done. I should have done this, I didn't do that." And he's asked why he didn't do it and he says: "I didn't think of it" or "I forgot" or "I was too busy." Damn, isn't that ineffective? Can you say I had effective representation? And now you have the judge saying this guy was a great lawyer, that he had extensive law enforcement experience, that he had handled twenty-seven capital cases. That's a lie. Literally, my case was the first case he'd handled in private practice—he had just left a public interest law firm.

Well, as a result these lawyers prepare very little —thanks to such small resources with which to prepare. Isn't it odd that you get that kind of lawyer at that point, appointed by the court? The court decides when that lawyer gets paid, *if* that lawyer gets paid, and how much that lawyer gets paid. So you have a lawyer who's beholden to the court for his fees. You get the worst possible legal help at the beginning of the process, but months or years later, after you're under a death warrant, you might be appointed three or four high-caliber Harvard-trained lawyers from one of the biggest law firms in the state—along with paralegals, investigators, psychologists? Does it strike you as an ass-backwards system? Well, that's the system that exists. That has been the lived experience of most men on death row. Is that a fair system? Why can't a man go to trial with the best lawyer if he's faced with death, rather than wait until he's under a death warrant?

AH: Tell us about a typical day here.

MAJ: A typical day begins at 6:25 a.m. A guard enters a "pod" of twenty-four men and announces "yard." "Yard list! Yard list!" If you're up, you can sign up by shouting out your number or your name. By 6:35, the morning meal arrives—a tray is delivered to your door. By 7:05, "yard" is allowed. "Yard" is a euphemism—it actually means "cage," because men go out into the cages here, being counted. You can go one, two, three, four at a time. That "yard" or "cage" period lasts for one hour. Then one goes back into his cell, and unless you have a visitor, you don't leave that cell until 7:05 the next morning. It's twenty-three hours lock-in, one hour outside, five days a week. On weekends, it's twenty-four hours lock-in. If you don't have a visitor, if you don't go to the law library—which is two hours, once or twice a week— you're in that cell.

AH: And nothing happens?

MAJ: Nothing happens unless you make it happen. Other than that, you're in that cell.

AH: So what do you do to hold up under those conditions?

MAJ: I'm an addicted writer and reader. I try to read everything I can get my paws on. I just finished reading two books by Alice Walker—*The*

Temple of My Familiar, and her most recent book. I've read Toni Morrison's *Jazz.* I've also read *Strange Justice* by Jane Mayer and Jill Abramson, on the confirmation hearings of Justice Clarence Thomas. I try to read as much as I can.

AH: How do you deal with the fact that you may be executed?

MAJ: I deal with it day to day. I mean, you can't, obviously, just dwell on that reality. You do the best you can every day to transform that reality into a new reality. Luckily, thanks to my book *Live from Death Row,* I have lawyers, very good lawyers, working on my case for the first time. So, you do your daily thing to keep well, to keep sane, to keep strong—to stay human.

AH: Do you feel that you've had an unusual share of bad luck?

MAJ: No, I really don't.

AH: Why have you attracted this fate, if I may put it that way?

MAJ: I think that I have a certain history, and because of my history, I have my share of enemies—political, governmental. How many people can brag—and I use that term with a little humor—about having an FBI file from the time they were fourteen? I have. Phone calls, mail, the whole deal—I've been tracked by the FBI since I was a

child. Dogged by them for my political beliefs, my
political expressions, my political associations.
If you were to review my FBI file, of course you'd
find a lot of nonsense in it because that's what FBI
files have in them. But you'd find an attempt by
the government, when I was perhaps seventeen or
eighteen years old, to frame me for two murders
in another country. What saved me was my work
record—my hourly work record showed that I not
only wasn't in that country, but that I was at work
doing what I was supposed to be doing. They also
tried to frame me when I went to college in Ver-
mont for a robbery of some sort. And I'm finding
this out reading these records years later.

AH: Are these publicly available records?

MAJ: Oh, yeah—through the Freedom of Information Act. You can contact my lawyers, and I'm sure
they can give you summaries or even copies of
some of them. We found roughly eight hundred
pages of FBI files—some blacked out, with whole
pages edited out. They wrote letters to people in
my name, signed them, sent them—letters that
were complete lies. This is what the government
admits to doing. And ultimately, what that record
says—not what I say, but what that record testi-
fies to—is a history of aggression. Not by me—you
can't look at that record and find any evidence
of any crime. But you can find lots of evidence of
government crimes against one of their so-called

"citizens" because of his political beliefs and associations. Because as a young man I spoke out as part of the Ministry of Information of the Black Panther Party. And I spoke about black liberation. That made me part of their target.

AH: Mumia, some would say you have the best of all possible worlds being in the United States. That you have the right to a representative jury, and you have the prohibition of the use of race as a bias in judicial proceedings. They'd say, go anywhere else in the world and you won't find it as good as you find it here.

MAJ: On some level, that's probably true. It's certainly true that that is the law as it is written. The question is, not what the law says, but what the law *does*—what the law is in application, not in just theoretical formulation. In the very real world—in the city of Philadelphia, with perhaps a 45 percent African-American population, many people like myself on death row have had an overwhelmingly white jury determine guilt or innocence, life or death. The U.S. Supreme Court has said countless times: "You can't do that." Well, they did that. They did it in my case, they did it in a number of people's cases. So it appears you *can* do that, because it happens every day. It happens every day because prosecutors routinely remove African-Americans from juries when they want a white jury, when it's a cross-racial case. So what it says on the books and what it actually means when one walks into the courtroom are often two different things.

In the famous case *Batson v. Kentucky* (it's relatively recent—1986, I believe) the Supreme Court required trial judges to assess a prosecutor's reasons for striking a minority juror, in order to determine whether he intended to discriminate. For years and years and years the late Justice Thurgood Marshall had been fighting for that principle. Justices across the country and lawyers had been fighting for that principle. Well, they won it in terms of that opinion; it's published in law books and sent to and taught in law schools. But what does it mean in the courtroom? *It means next to nothing.* Because you still have a predominantly white judiciary that protects the power class, that looks at the situation and looks the other way. About fifty miles from here in the city of Pittsburgh, there's a case that's stirring a great deal of controversy, because of a Judge Manning of the Court of Common Pleas of Pittsburgh, Allegheny County. Five witnesses have testified that Justice Manning—in a nonjudicial setting, but a public setting nonetheless—spoke to a woman who was a security guard at an airport thusly: "That's what happens when you give a fucking nigger a job." These are white people who claim this guy said that. I don't know if he said it or not, but you have five eyewitnesses who swore in statements that this judge of the Court of Common Pleas said it. My point is: What does that translate to when that judge is sitting in office, in his robes, and he has a defendant in front of him who looks like me, and he has to decide what his jury looks like? What does it mean if that judge becomes a Supreme Court justice? And what does it really mean, and what does it matter, what is written in the books—if what's written in the hearts and minds and souls of people is still, in the words of Justice Taney, that a black man "has no rights that a white man is bound to respect?"

In terms of *Batson,* the evidence in my case is just so clear, so insurmountable. In the context not so much of what happened at the trial, but what happened at last summer's Petition for Post-Conviction Relief hearings in Philadelphia, where we found out that the Commonwealth agreed that the jury numbers they presented to the Supreme Court on direct appeal were wrong. They said eight African-Americans were removed from my original jury; my lawyer on appeal said eleven were removed. Well, we found two of those persons. We couldn't find the third one, but we found two. So they had to admit, "OK, we were wrong, ten were removed." So it was ten out of fourteen. Now, my math is very poor, but I think it's at least 71 percent of potential African-Americans that were excluded on the basis of race. There are cases that say if you can show a 56 percent removal rate, you have a *prima facie Batson* claim. . . .

AH: You have said that you "live in the fast-est-growing public housing tract in America."

MAJ: I do.

AH: You've described torture, theft, terror, humil-iation, degradation, brutality. Do you stand by all that?

MAJ: Absolutely. A lot of people who don't know this reality have perhaps read my book *Live from Death Row* and reacted to it with complete incre-dulity. The reality is that my book is a toned-down, stripped, bare-bones, objective version of the reali-ty I'm living on death row, in the hole—of what I've seen, what I've smelt; the bodies I've seen carried out of here.

If I wrote pure stream of consciousness, no pub-lisher would publish it, and any reader would say it's fiction. The reality is that this is a world that is, by design, closed. Were it not for a court order and our civil action, this very interview would not have transpired. Six months ago, it would not have been allowed. As we speak, the state of California has announced a moratorium on all interviews with all prisoners throughout the penal system. There's a reason for that. It's to keep people in the dark.

AH: Mumia, thank you for talking with us today.

The prison official signals that our time is up; then a guard comes into Mumia's side of the cubicle and motions for him to follow. Mumia raises his cuffed hands in a kind of salute, his eyes fixed on us, and says in a loud, cheerful voice: "Ona move!" He then turns and goes out. As do all Pennsylvania death row inmates before and after a visit, Mumia will endure a body-cavity strip search before returning to the isolation of his cell. Meanwhile, we banter with the prison administrator as we pack up our gear and walk back through the quiet, lonely corridors. She tells us of her twelve-year-old son, and how she does not want him to ever work in prisons.

Waynesburg, PA
February 8, 1996

A LIFE IN THE BALANCE—
THE CASE OF MUMIA ABU-JAMAL

By Amnesty International
Originally released on February 17, 2000
AI Index: AMR 51/01/99

Introduction

Mumia Abu-Jamal has been incarcerated on Pennsylvania's death row for the past 17 years. His case has generated more controversy and received more attention, both national and international, than that of any other inmate currently under sentence of death in the United States of America (USA).

Mumia Abu-Jamal, black, was convicted and sentenced to death in July 1982 for the murder of white police officer Daniel Faulkner on December 9, 1981. He has steadfastly maintained his innocence since 1981. Since the trial, those advocating his release or retrial have contested the validity of much of the evidence used to obtain his conviction. These accusations have been countered by members of the law enforcement community and their supporters, who have agitated for Mumia Abu-Jamal's execution while maintaining that the trial was unbiased and fair.

In light of the contradictory and incomplete evidence in this case, Amnesty International can take no position on the guilt or innocence of Mumia Abu-Jamal. Nor has the organization identified him as a political prisoner, although it has previously expressed its concern over the activities of a government counterintelligence program, which appeared to number Abu-Jamal among its targets. However, the organization is concerned that political statements attributed to him as a teenager were improperly used by the prosecution in its efforts to obtain a death sentence against him. In any event, the administration of the death penalty in the USA remains a highly politicized affair, sanctioned and supported by elected officials for its perceived political advantages. The politicization of Mumia Abu-Jamal's case may not only have prejudiced his right to a fair trial, but may now be undermining his right to fair and impartial treatment in the appeal courts.

After many years of monitoring Mumia Abu-Jamal's case and a thorough study of original documents, including the entire trial transcript, the organization has concluded that the proceedings used to convict and sentence Mumia Abu-Jamal to death were in violation of minimum international standards that govern fair trial procedures and the use of the death penalty. Amnesty International therefore believes that the interests of justice would best be served by the granting of a new trial to Mumia Abu-Jamal (see conclusion).

In October 1999, Abu-Jamal filed his initial federal appeal. The federal courts represent Abu-Jamal's final opportunity to have many of the troubling issues in his case addressed and corrected. However, as discussed below, the 1996 Anti-terrorism and Effective Death Penalty Act severely limits the federal courts' ability to ensure that legal proceedings at the state level guaranteed the defendants' rights enshrined in the US Constitution and under international human rights standards. Amnesty International has chosen this time, a time when Abu-Jamal's life is in the balance, to release this report.

Mumia Abu-Jamal is one of more than three and a half thousand people on death row in 37 states and under federal law throughout the USA. By the end of 1999, 598 prisoners had been put to death in 30 states since executions resumed in 1977; in 1999 alone, 98 prisoners died at the hands of the state, a record year since the 1950s. The US authorities have repeatedly violated international minimum safeguards in their continuing resort to capital punishment. Violations include the execution of the mentally impaired, of child offenders, and of those who received inadequate legal representation at trial. Those sentenced to death in the USA are overwhelmingly the poor, and disproportionately come from racial and ethnic minority communities. The risk of wrongful conviction remains high, with more than 80 prisoners released from death rows since 1973 after evidence of their innocence emerged. Many came close to execution before the courts acted on their claims of wrongful conviction. Others have gone to their deaths despite serious doubts concerning their guilt.

Amnesty International unconditionally opposes the death penalty under all circumstances. Even if it were possible for a country to create a judicial system entirely fair and free from bias and error, the punishment of death would still violate the most fundamental of all human rights. Each death sentence and execution is an affront to human dignity: the ultimate form of cruel, inhuman and degrading punishment.

In opposing the death penalty, Amnesty International in no way seeks to minimize or condone the crimes for which those sentenced to death and executed were convicted. Nor does the organization seek to belittle the appalling suffering of the families of murder victims, for whom it has the greatest sympathy. However, the finality and cruelty inherent in the death penalty render it incompatible with norms of modern-day civilized behaviour and an inappropriate and unacceptable response to violent crime.

The continued and accelerating use of the death penalty is one of many serious human rights violations that Amnesty International has identified and repeatedly raised with the US authorities. These other concerns include a nationwide pattern of police brutality; the physical and sexual abuse of prisoners, inhuman or degrading conditions of confinement and the mistreatment of asylum seekers.[1]

The backdrop: Philadelphia, a city of racial tensions, police brutality and police corruption

The shooting of Officer Daniel Faulkner in 1981 and Mumia Abu-Jamal's trial the following year took place in Philadelphia, a city fraught with tension between the predominantly white authorities and the African American and other minority communities. Both before and since that time, numerous instances have come to light of police brutality and the use of disproportionate force with lethal consequences; of the corruption of police officers and the fabrication of evidence against those suspected of criminal acts.[2]

In 1973, a federal judge for the US District Court stated that police abuse occurred with such frequency in Philadelphia that it could not be "dismissed as rare, isolated instances" and that city officials did "little or nothing" to punish or prevent police abuse.

In 1979, the US Department of Justice filed a lawsuit against the then-mayor of Philadelphia, Frank Rizzo, and other city officials for condoning police brutality. The lawsuit listed 290 persons shot by the city's police officers between 1975 and 1979, the majority of whom were from ethnic minorities. During Frank Rizzo's eight years as mayor, fatal shootings by Philadelphia police officers increased by 20 per cent annually. In the year after he left office, 1980, fatal shootings declined 67 per cent.[3] Mayor Rizzo appeared to tolerate police misconduct. In 1978, he told an audience of 700 police officers "Even when you're wrong, I'm going to back you."[4]

An investigation in 1978 by the Pennsylvania House of Representatives Sub-Committee on Crime and Corrections found that a small but significant number of Philadelphia police routinely engaged in verbal and physical abuse of citizens to a degree the subcommittee considered "lawless." The investigation concluded that the level of police abuse had reached that of homicidal violence and that Philadelphia lacked the necessary police leadership to control the lawlessness.

Also in 1978, the police became involved in a siege of a house occupied by members of MOVE.[5] During an attempt to force the occupants to leave the building a shot was fired, causing the police to open fire at the house (it is disputed whether the police or those in the house fired the initial shot). At this time, one police officer was fatally wounded; MOVE members later maintained that the police officer was killed by gunfire from other officers. As the occupants surrendered to the police, television cameras filmed a police officer striking Delbert Africa (all members of MOVE adopt the second name of Africa) with the butt of a shotgun and then dragging him along the ground as other police officers kicked him. Police bulldozed the house to the ground the following day, destroying the crime scene and making analysis of many of the day's events impossible.[6] Nine members of MOVE were tried on charges of third-degree murder, conspiracy, and multiple counts of attempted murder and aggravated assault; all were found guilty and sentenced to 30 to 100 years in prison.

Mumia Abu-Jamal was closely involved with MOVE. It is highly likely that the officers who arrested him, although perhaps unaware of his identity, would have immediately associated him with the organization because of his dreadlocks, a hairstyle adopted by all members of MOVE as part of their beliefs. Abu-Jamal was also a former member of the Black Panther Party (BPP) and was under surveillance by the FBI's Counterintelligence Program, COINTELPRO.[7] Prior to his arrest, Abu-Jamal worked as a journalist and had written articles critical of the authorities in Philadelphia. To supplement his income, he was working as a taxi cab driver at the time of the crime.

The crime: the shooting of police officer Daniel Faulkner
On December 9, 1981, at approximately 3:55 a.m., Officer Daniel Faulkner of the Philadelphia Police Department stopped a car driven by Mumia Abu-Jamal's brother, William Cook. A struggle ensued between the two men. Mumia Abu-Jamal, who was driving a cab in the vicinity, observed his brother in an altercation with the officer and got out of his vehicle. Minutes later, more police officers arrived on the scene to find Officer Faulkner dead from two bullet wounds to the head and back.

Mumia Abu-Jamal was sitting nearby wounded in the chest by a bullet from the police officer's gun. Abu-Jamal's own legally registered gun was found a few feet away from where he sat.

Media coverage of the case as it proceeded to trial referred extensively to Abu-Jamal's affiliations with MOVE and his former membership in the Black Panther Party. The continual references to Abu-Jamal's past political activities caused Joe Davidson, president of the Association of Black Journalists to state "[w]e are disturbed by disparaging news reports about Mr. Jamal's political and religious beliefs. As an organization dedicated to truth and fairness in journalism, we will continue to monitor media coverage on this matter. We hope that Mr. Jamal will be tried in the courtroom and not in the press."[8] Following investigations by the authorities, pretrial hearings in the case began on January 5, 1982. On June 7, 1982, the trial of Mumia Abu-Jamal on a charge of first degree murder and possession of an instrument of crime commenced in Philadelphia, amid intense publicity.

The trial judge: an independent and fair arbiter of justice?

"The judiciary shall decide matters before them impartially, on the basis of the facts and in accordance with the law, without restrictions, improper influences, inducements, pressure, threats or interferences, direct or indirect, from any quarter or for any reason."[9]

Where a defendant has selected trial by jury, the ultimate disposition of the case rests with the jurors and not with court

officials. But the overall conduct of the trial is the responsibility of the presiding judge, and jurors look to the judge for
guidance and instruction on the complex legal issues before
them. Any hint of bias from the bench may thus have a profound effect on the jury's deliberations.

The trial of Mumia Abu-Jamal was presided over by Judge
Albert F. Sabo. His history of involvement with the police and
law enforcement community has raised concerns that he was
not the most suitable choice of officials to oversee the trial of a
defendant accused of killing a police officer. Albert Sabo was an
Undersheriff of Philadelphia County for 16 years before becoming a judge in 1974. His official biography lists him as a former
member of the National Sheriffs' Association, "retired Fraternal
Order of Police" (FOP) and as associated with the Police Chiefs'
Association of South East Pennsylvania.[10] As a judge he was
no stranger to the death penalty. Over a period of 14 years, he
presided over trials in which 31 defendants were sentenced to
death, more than any other US judge as far as Amnesty International is aware. Of the 31 condemned defendants, 29 came from
ethnic minorities.[11]

The judicial conduct of Judge Sabo has been a cause for
concern to many members of the Philadelphia legal community
for a number of years. A 1983 Philadelphia Bar survey found
that over one-third of the responding attorneys considered
Judge Sabo unqualified to be on the bench. When asked about
the survey, Judge Sabo appeared to reveal his bias against the
defense by stating that if he were a defense attorney "I wouldn't
vote for me either."

In 1992 the *Philadelphia Inquirer* reviewed 35 homicide trials presided over by Judge Sabo.[12] The investigation concluded that: "through his comments, his rulings and his instructions to the jury" Judge Sabo "favored prosecutors." According to the report, in one case, Judge Sabo even urged the prosecution to introduce evidence because "it would be helpful to [get] a conviction." A review of the court records by the *Inquirer* showed "that most of the homicide judges in Philadelphia hear more murder cases than Judge Sabo with fewer death sentences." In the same article, the *Inquirer* also concluded: "The assignment of a judge, like the naming of a lawyer, can be a life-or-death matter for a murder suspect. Some, like Judge Albert F. Sabo, are viewed as prosecution-minded. Others are seen as more favorable to defense. One report likened the system to a 'crap shoot'."

Throughout Abu-Jamal's trial—a trial to determine whether the defendant would live or die—Judge Sabo appeared to be more concerned with expediency than fairness. For example, during the proceedings of June 17, he stated "I don't want to be held up on lousy technicalities . . . what do I care?" and "As far as I'm concerned, it can wait until lunchtime. Whatever you want to do, but let's do something. I have a jury waiting out there."

In 1995, defense lawyers requested that Judge Sabo recuse (i.e. remove) himself from presiding over an evidentiary hearing on whether Mumia Abu-Jamal's original trial was fair, on the grounds of "his inability to endow this proceeding with . . . the appearance of fairness and impartiality." Judge Sabo refused. During the hearing, he was openly hostile to the defense, causing one commentator to write: "[t]hroughout the internationally scrutinized post-conviction hearing, which ran from July 26 to August 15, and the closing arguments on September 11,

Judge Sabo flaunted his bias, oozing partiality toward the prosecution and crudely seeking to bully Weinglass [a defense lawyer], whose courtroom conduct was as correct as Sabo's was crass."[13] On July 16, 1996, the *Philadelphia Inquirer* described Judge Sabo's adjudication of the hearings: "The behavior of the judge was disturbing first time around—and in hearings last week he did not give the impression to those in the courtroom of fair-mindedness. Instead, he gave the impression, damaging in the extreme, of undue haste and hostility toward the defense's case."

The defense: Mumia Abu-Jamal's legal representation at trial

"They [defense lawyers] must aid their clients in every appropriate way, taking such actions as is necessary to protect their clients' rights and interests, and assist their clients before the courts."[14]

US death penalty procedures are a uniquely complex area of criminal law, in which even attorneys experienced in non-capital trials may fail to adequately represent their clients. Amnesty International has documented numerous cases of death row prisoners who were represented at trial by woefully inadequate defense attorneys.[15] Its concern over such cases is shared by other international human rights groups and inter-governmental bodies. In 1996, for example, the International Commission of Jurists (ICJ), an international non-governmental organization which takes no position on the death penalty per se, published a report that was highly critical of the legal representation afforded defendants in capital cases, concluding: "the administration of the death penalty in the United States will remain arbitrary, and racially discriminatory, and prospects of a fair hearing for capital offenders cannot (and will not) be assured" without substantial remedial steps.[16] The UN Human Rights Committee (HRC—the expert body empowered to monitor countries' compliance with the International Covent on Civil and Political Rights—the ICCPR) has also made note of the concern over the "the lack of effective measures [in the USA] to ensure that indigent [poor] defendants inserious criminal proceedings, particularly in state courts, are represented by competent counsel."[17]

At the time of Mumia Abu-Jamal's trial, Pennsylvania had no minimum standards for those appointed to represent defendants on trial for their life. Attorneys in capital cases were not required to pass any special examinations or to have reached any level of experience in defending those facing trial on serious charges.[18]

Mumia Abu-Jamal was initially represented by a court-appointed attorney, Anthony Jackson. At a pretrial hearing on May 13, 1982, Abu-Jamal requested the court's permission to represent himself at trial because he was dissatisfied with Jackson's performance.[19] Judge Ribner, the judge overseeing the pretrial hearings, granted his request but, over Abu-Jamal's vigorous objection, appointed Jackson as backup counsel. Jackson also protested at being appointed as backup counsel, stating that he did not know what it entailed, but was told by the judge; "You can fight that out with Mr. Jamal." Jackson was given no clarification by the court as to his role in the trial as backup counsel.

Since Mumia Abu-Jamal was obviously unable to conduct investigations due to his continued detention, his access to a fully prepared lawyer—even as "backup counsel"—was vital to ensure a fair hearing. In a sworn affidavit dated April 17, 1995, Jackson admitted to being "unprepared" for trial and that he "abandoned all efforts at trial preparation" three weeks before the start of the trial after Mumia Abu-Jamal had obtained the right to represent himself.

During jury selection on the third day of the trial, at the suggestion of the prosecution, Judge Sabo withdrew permission for Mumia Abu-Jamal to act as his own attorney—supposedly only for the duration of jury selection. Judge Sabo based this decision on Abu-Jamal's alleged slowness in questioning potential jurors and on the grounds that his status as an accused murderer instilled fear and anxiety in the jurors. However, Judge Sabo did concede that ". . . it is true I have not rebuked Mr. Jamal at any time [during jury selection]."

Jackson objected to the ruling, pointing out to Judge Sabo that "The last case I had before you, it took us nine days to select a jury and it certainly didn't have as much publicity as this case." Jackson noted that jury selection in another homicide case had taken five weeks to complete. He went on to state that "in all homicide cases, particularly in capital cases . . . jurors express some apprehension, some unsettlement, some fear with regard to the whole process." These objections were to no avail, Judge Sabo continued to deny Abu-Jamal the right to represent himself.

The *Philadelphia Inquirer* described Abu-Jamal's conduct prior to his removal as lead counsel as "intent and business like" and "subdued." In the first two days of the trial, Abu-Jamal had questioned 23 prospective jurors, successfully challenging two for "cause" (bias), defeating a prosecution challenge for cause, and exercising two peremptory strikes (the right to remove a prospective juror without giving reasons).

Amnesty International's own examination of the trial transcript found no justifiable reason for the revoking of Mumia Abu-Jamal's right to question potential jurors. At no point during his questioning was he rude or aggressive and his examinations are very similar, in terms of length, to those of the prosecution. His questions were pertinent to the selection of a fair jury. The removal of Abu-Jamal's right to represent himself at this point in the trial is not supported in any way by the record of the trial. Judge Sabo's comment that "You have indicated to this court that you do not have the expertise necessary to conduct *voir dire*" (jury selection) is likewise not supported by the record.

After the jury had been selected and the trial proper began, Mumia Abu-Jamal resumed representing himself. However, the already tense relations between him and Judge Sabo deteriorated rapidly. It is clear from the exchanges between the two men that Abu-Jamal had come to the conclusion that he would be denied a fair trial by the court. His repeated requests to be legally represented by John Africa were denied by Judge Sabo, on the grounds that Africa was not a licensed attorney.[20] Mumia Abu-Jamal also requested that John Africa be allowed to sit at the defense table, in order to provide legal and tactical advice throughout the trial. This request was permissible under Pennsylvania law but was denied by Judge Sabo. When pressed by

Abu-Jamal, who gave examples of other judges who had allowed non-lawyers to sit at the table of defendants, Judge Sabo stated that unless there was a legal precedent, he did not care what other judges did, and continued to refuse the request. Typical of the exchanges between Judge Sabo and Mumia Abu-Jamal is the following:

Judge Sabo: *Mr. Jamal, it is quite evident to this court that you are intentionally disrupting the orderly procedure of this court. I have warned you time and again that if you continue with that attitude that I would have to remove you as counsel in this case.*

Mumia Abu-Jamal: *Judge, your warnings to me are absolutely meaningless. I'm here fighting for my life. Do you understand that? I'm not fighting to please the Court, or to please the DA, I'm fighting for my life. I need counsel of choice, someone I have faith in, someone I have respect for; not someone paid by the same pocket that pays the DA, not a court-appointed lawyer, not a member of the ABA, not an officer of the court but someone I can trust and I have faith in. Your warnings are absolutely moot, they're meaningless to me.*

Shortly after this exchange, Judge Sabo prohibited Mumia Abu-Jamal from representing himself in court and Jackson was reappointed lead counsel. Jackson protested, but his request to be removed was rejected by Judge Sabo, who threatened the lawyer with disciplinary action, including imprisonment for contempt of court, unless he continued.[21] This left the defendant represented by a lawyer who was both reluctant to participate and ill-prepared for trial, effectively stripping Mumia Abu-Jamal of any meaningful legal representation. The following day, after a number of other angry exchanges between judge and defendant, Judge Sabo had Abu-Jamal physically removed from the courtroom.

For the remainder of the trial, Mumia Abu-Jamal was continuously readmitted to and removed from the trial. His behavior in the courtroom became highly belligerent and disruptive to the proceedings, leaving Judge Sabo with little choice but to remove him if the trial were to continue. However, even if his behavior justified the court in excluding Abu-Jamal from many of the critical parts of the trial, it would not release the presiding authorities from the duty to conduct a fair and impartial trial and from ensuring that his exclusion infringed as little as possible on Abu-Jamal's right to participate in his own defense. In effect, Mumia Abu-Jamal was tried in absentia during a large portion of the trial.

The right to the resources necessary for an adequate defense

During the proceedings, every person is entitled . . . to obtain the appearance, as witnesses, of experts or other persons who may throw light on the facts.[22]

Mumia Abu-Jamal's lack of meaningful legal representation was compounded by the refusal of Judge Ribner, the pretrial judge, to grant the defense adequate funds to employ an investigator, pathologist or ballistics expert. The court also

refused defense attorney Jackson's requests for a second attorney to aid the defense.[23] In response to the initial request
for funds, the Court allocated $150 for each expert. On three
occasions, the defense attempted to have this amount increased as it was proving impossible to obtain expert evaluation of the evidence for this fee. On each occasion this
entirely reasonable request was denied. Jackson explained to
Judge Ribner that he was experiencing difficulties in recruit-
ing the experts without the guarantee of funding. The judge
replied that if Jackson submitted an itemized bill for the work
the judge would approve payment, assuming he found the
charges reasonable. Jackson pointed out that he had told the
experts this but that they were still not willing to work without an advance payment—to which the judge replied: "Tell
them, 'The Calendar judge said 'trust me'."[24]

This sum allocated by the courts to cover Jackson's fees
and expenses for his work on the case for over six months, payment for an investigator to locate and interview witnesses, and
fees for experts to evaluate the evidence and testify in court
concerning their findings, was clearly insufficient. The defense
presented **no** expert testimony on ballistics or pathology.[25] The
police and prosecution interviewed more than 100 witnesses
during their investigation of the crime. The evaluation of these
statements alone would have taken more time than Jackson
could afford to devote to them.

The jury: a fair and impartial panel of Abu-Jamal's peers?
An essential element of a fair trial is the selection of an impar-

tial jury of the defendant's peers, one which will base its verdict solely on the evidence presented to it. Where a case generates a high degree of controversy and publicity, trial courts routinely grant a change of venue, to ensure that the jury has not been exposed to pretrial publicity that could bias its deliberations. Of approximately 80 people in the jury pool at Mumia Abu-Jamal's trial, all but seven prospective jurors admitted that they were familiar with media coverage of the case.

The jury eventually selected (including the four alternate jurors[26]) consisted of two blacks and 14 whites. The population of Philadelphia at the time of the trial was 40 per cent African American; a jury racially representative of the community could thus have been expected to include at least five black members.

The prosecution used 11 out of its 15 peremptory strikes to remove African Americans from the jury. In 1986, the US Supreme Court ruled in the case of *Batson v. Kentucky* that the removal of potential jurors must be "race neutral."[27]

The jurors selected for the trial of Mumia Abu-Jamal appear to have received different treatment from the court according to their race. Jennie Dawley, black, was the only juror selected while Abu-Jamal was conducting his own defense. Dawley requested, before the trial started, that she be allowed to take her sick cat to the veterinarian during the evening, thereby not disrupting the court proceedings.[28] Judge Sabo denied this request without informing the defense. Juror Dawley was dismissed from the jury when she failed to abide by the Court's instruction. In contrast, a white juror requested permission to take a civil service exam during court time. Judge Sabo granted this request, temporarily halted the trial and instructed a court official to accompany the juror and ensure that he saw no media coverage of the trial.

Jennie Dawley was replaced by a white alternate juror, Robert Courchain. On at least five occasions during jury selection, Courchain stated that, although he would try, he might be unable to set aside his bias in the case. For example, he stated: "unconsciously I don't think I could be fair to both sides." The defense sought the removal of Courchain "for cause" (i.e. that he was incapable of deliberating impartially), but Judge Sabo denied the request. As Jackson had previously used the one peremptory strike available to him at this point he was unable to prevent Courchain from becoming an alternate juror.

Jackson also allowed two jurors onto the jury whose life experiences could possibly prejudice them against Abu-Jamal. Juror number 11 was the close friend of a police officer who had been shot while on duty. While being questioned, he openly admitted that this experience could mean he was unable to be a fair juror because of his feelings concerning his friend. Juror number 15 (an alternate) was the wife of a serving police officer. Jackson allowed both onto the jury without objection.

The case for the prosecution: too many unresolved questions

At trial, the prosecution's case against Abu-Jamal consisted of three elements:

—the "confession" allegedly made by Abu-Jamal at the hospital;

—three eyewitnesses who testified that they saw Abu-Jamal commit the offense;

—the presence of Abu-Jamal's gun at the murder scene, which the prosecution alleged was the murder weapon.

Mumia Abu-Jamal's "confession"

"One can have eyewitness testimonial evidence, circumstantial evidence, scientific evidence, and even video evidence; but a confession explicitly admitting guilt . . . is the most powerful piece of evidence that can ever be introduced against him and will surely serve as the key that locks the jail-house door and provides the juice to power the electric chair; and in these more civilized times, the juice for the needle." Judge Overstreet, Texas Court of Criminal Appeals.[29]

During the trial, the jury heard testimony from hospital security guard Priscilla Durham and police officer Gary Bell.[30] According to both witnesses, when about to receive treatment for his bullet wound at the hospital, Mumia Abu-Jamal stated: "I shot the motherfucker, and I hope the motherfucker dies."

During an appeal court hearing in 1995, a third witness, police officer Gary Wakshul, also claimed to have heard the statement. However, Officer Wakshul, who was in the police vehicle that took Mumia Abu-Jamal to the hospital, had written in his report that "we stayed with the male at Jefferson [hospital] until we were relieved. During this time, the negro male made no comments."

None of the many other police officers in and around the hospital treatment room at that time claimed to have heard the statement, which Abu-Jamal allegedly shouted. Doctors who treated Abu-Jamal at the hospital stated in their testimony that they were with him from the moment he arrived, that he was "weak . . . on the verge of fainting," and that they did not hear him make any statement that could be interpreted as a confession.

None of the three witnesses to the alleged confession reported what they had claimed to have heard until February 1982, more than two months after the shooting. They reported the alleged incriminating statements during interviews with the police Internal Affairs Unit. The interviews took place after Abu-Jamal made allegations of being abused by the police when he was arrested.[31] Officer Wakshul claimed that his delay in reporting the confession was due to "emotional trauma" caused by the murder of Officer Faulkner. The two other witnesses stated that they did not believe the outburst was significant enough to report to the police.

However, during her trial testimony, Priscilla Durham claimed that she had reported the statement to her hospital supervisor the day after the events and that they had prepared a handwritten note of her allegation. Upon hearing this testimony, the prosecution sent an officer to the hospital in an attempt to recover the supervisor's record of Durham's statement. The officer returned from the hospital with an unsigned typewritten statement, which Priscilla Durham denied having seen before. Despite finding that this was not the original document, that the witness had not seen it before that day, and that its authenticity was not verified, Judge Sabo allowed it into evidence. He conjectured that "They took the handwritten statement and typed this"—events that were not in evidence and that he was thus not in a position to deduce.

Gary Wakshul, the officer who noted in his report that "during this time, the male negro made no statements," did not testify at the trial. When the defense lawyer attempted to call him as a witness, it transpired that he was on holiday, despite a notation on a police investigation report that Wakshul was not permitted to be on leave at the time of the trial. The defense requested that Officer Wakshul's whereabouts be established or that the trial be temporarily halted to enable them to locate him. That request was denied by Judge Sabo, who commented to Mumia Abu-Jamal that "your attorney and you goofed."

The jury was never informed of the existence of Officer Wakshul's written report of his custody of Mumia Abu-Jamal which clearly contradicts the claim that the suspect "confessed" to killing Officer Faulkner. Therefore, the jury was left with little reason to doubt the testimony of the two witnesses who claimed to have heard the confession.

The likelihood of two police officers and a security guard forgetting or neglecting to report the confession of a suspect in the killing of another police officer for more than two months strains credulity. Priscilla Durham's claim that she believed Mumia Abu-Jamal's "confession" was important enough to report to her supervisor (who in turn thought it important enough to have typed out from the original handwritten version) but not important enough to notify the police is scarcely credible.

In a conversation with an Amnesty International researcher, one of Mumia Abu-Jamal's current legal team stated that a number of the jurors have told defense investigators that they had taken into consideration Abu-Jamal's "confession," not just in deciding his guilt but also in sentencing him to death, since the statement portrayed him as aggressive and callous. However, the jurors refused to make any public statements to this effect.

The concern remains that a possibly fabricated "confession" may have been a major contributing factor in the jury sentencing Mumia Abu-Jamal to death.

Witnesses to the crime: conflicting and confusing

During the trial, three witnesses testified that Abu-Jamal had run up to Officer Faulkner, shot him in the back and then stood over him and fired another bullet into his head, killing him instantly (although only one witness, White, claimed to have seen the events as described above in their entirety). None of the witnesses testified that Faulkner fired at Abu-Jamal as he fell to the ground—even when specifically asked—as the prosecution maintained. The prosecution also maintained that only Abu-Jamal, his brother William Cook and Officer Faulkner were present in the immediate vicinity of the crime scene.

In the years since the trial, defense lawyers have thrown into doubt the reliability of much of this trial testimony.

The complicated nature of the numerous accusations, counter-accusations and withdrawing of statements and testimony make it impossible, based on the existing record, to reach definitive conclusions regarding the reliability of any witness. The prosecutors and police contend that the testimony presented at the trial was truthful and uncoerced, and that other witnesses to the crime were not called to testify as they had nothing relevant to add.

However, Abu-Jamal's attorneys contend that a number of witnesses changed their original statements regarding what they saw on the night of the crime after being coerced, threatened or offered inducements by the police. Based on a comparison of their statements given to the police immediately after the shooting, their testimony during pretrial hearings and their testimony at the trial, the key witnesses did substantively alter their descriptions of what they saw, in ways that supported the prosecution's version of events.

Cynthia White and Veronica Jones

Cynthia White was a prostitute working in the area on the night in question. At the trial she testified that she had seen Mumia Abu-Jamal run up to Officer Faulkner, shoot him in the back, and then stand over him firing at his head.

Prior to the trial, White had given four written statements and one tape-recorded statement to the police. In one interview she estimated the height of the person who shot Faulkner to be shorter than five feet eight inches. Abu-Jamal is six feet one inch tall. In her first court appearance at a pretrial hearing, she testified that Abu-Jamal held the gun in his left hand. Three days later she testified that she was unsure which hand he held the gun in. At trial she denied knowing which hand the gun was in. During her trial testimony, she claimed that the diagram she originally drew of the incident was incorrect and that her placement of the actors prior to Abu-Jamal's appearance was inaccurate.

There is evidence to show that Cynthia White received preferential treatment from the prosecution and police. At the time of the trial, she was serving an 18-month prison sentence for prostitution in Massachusetts. She had 38 previous arrests for prostitution in Philadelphia; three of those charges were still pending at the time of trial. She was arrested twice within days of the shooting incident (December 12 and 17). According to Abu-Jamal's current defense attorneys, there are no records of White ever being prosecuted for those arrests.

In 1987, a detective involved in the prosecution of Abu-Jamal testified in support of bail for White at a court hearing concerning charges of robbery, aggravated assault and possession of illegal weapons. Despite the judge pointing out that White had failed to appear in court on 17 different occasions and that she had "page after page" of arrests and convictions, the prosecution consented to the request that she be allowed to sign her own bail and the judge released her. According to information received by Amnesty International, White failed to appear in court on the charges and the authorities have since been unable to locate her. At an appeal hearings in 1997, the prosecution claimed Cynthia White was deceased and produced a 1992 death certificate in the name of Cynthia Williams, claiming that the fingerprints of the dead woman and White matched. However, an examination of the fingerprint records of White and Williams showed no match and the evidence that White is now dead is far from conclusive.

A second prostitute, Veronica Jones, witnessed the killing and testified for the defense. She claimed she had been offered inducements by the police to testify that she saw Abu-Jamal kill Faulkner, stating that "they [the police] were trying to get me to say something the other girl [White] said. I couldn't do that." Jones went on to testify that "they [the police] told us we could work the area [as prostitutes] if we tell them [that Abu-Jamal was the shooter]."

However, Judge Sabo had the jury removed for this testimony and then ruled that Jones's statements were inadmissible evidence. The jury were thus left unaware of the allegations that police officers were offering inducements in return for testimony against Abu-Jamal. In her testimony before the jury, Jones retracted her original statement to police that she saw two unidentified men leave the scene of the crime. Remarkably, Jackson had never interviewed his own witness (a standard practice) but Jones was interviewed by the prosecution prior to the trial.

In 1996, Veronica Jones testified at an appeal hearing that she changed her version of events after being visited by two police officers in prison, where she was being held on charges of robbery and assault. While cross-examining Jones, the prosecution announced to the court that there was an outstanding arrest warrant for Jones on charges of passing bad checks and indicated that she would be arrested at the conclusion of her testimony.

In a sworn affidavit, Jones described her meeting with the plain clothes police officers:

> They told me that if I would testify against Jamal and identify Jamal as the shooter I wouldn't have to worry about my pending felony charges. . . . The detectives threatened me by reminding me that I faced a long prison sentence—fifteen years. . . . I knew that if I did anything to help the Jamal defense I would face years in prison.

After Abu-Jamal's trial, Veronica Jones received a sentence of two years' probation on the charges she was facing.

In January 1997, another former prostitute who worked in

the area of the crime scene in 1981, came forward. In a sworn affidavit, Pamela Jenkins stated that she knew Cynthia White, who had told her she was afraid of the police and that the police were trying to get her to say something about the shooting of Faulkner and had threatened her life. Jenkins was the lover and informant of Philadelphia police officer Tom Ryan. In her statement, Jenkins claimed that Ryan "wanted me to perjure myself and say that I had seen Jamal shoot the police officer." In 1996, Tom Ryan and five other officers from the same district went to prison after being convicted of charges of planting evidence, stealing money from suspects and making false reports. Their convictions resulted in the release of numerous prisoners implicated by the officers. Jenkins was a principal prosecution witness at the trials of the officers.

Robert Chobert

Robert Chobert had just let a passenger out of his cab and was parked when he viewed the incident. It is undisputed that he was closest to the scene of the prosecution eyewitnesses, parked in his cab a car's length behind Faulkner's police car and approximately 50 feet from the shooting. According to his testimony and statements, he was writing in his logbook when he heard the first shot and looked up. He had to look over or past Faulkner's car, with its flashing red dome light, to see the incident and saw the shooter only in profile. Chobert testified at trial that when he looked up, he saw Faulkner fall and then saw Abu-Jamal "standing over him and firing some more shots into him." Under cross-examination by Jackson, he stated: "I know who shot the cop, and I ain't going to forget it."

But Chobert's first recorded statement to police—about

which the jury was not told—was that the shooter "apparent-ly ran away," according to a report written on December 10, 1981, by Inspector Giordano. Giordano encountered Chobert upon reaching the scene about five minutes after the shooting. Giordano wrote: "[A] white male from the crowd stated that he saw the shooting and that a black MOVE member had done it and appearently [sic] ran away. When asked what he ment [sic] bby [sic] a MOVE member, the white male stated, 'His hair, his hair,' appearantly [sic] referring to dreadlocks."

There are also discrepancies between Chobert's descrip-tion of the shooter's clothes and weight and that of Abu-Jamal.

During the trial, Jackson attempted to introduce into evi-dence Chobert's previous convictions for driving while intox-icated (twice) and the arson of a school, for which he was on probation. Jackson sought to introduce the convictions to chal-lenge Chobert's credibility, but Judge Sabo refused to allow the defense the opportunity to make the jury aware of Chobert's convictions.

The jury were also left unaware that Chobert had been driv-ing his cab with a suspended driver's license on the night of the killing, that it was still suspended at the time of the trial, and that the police had never sought to charge him for this offense. According to Chobert's testimony at the 1995 hearing, he had asked the prosecutor during the trial "if he could help me find out how I could get my license back," which was "important" to him because "that's how I earned my living." According to Chobert, the prosecutor told him that he would "look into it."

During this final summation to the jury, the prosecutor em-phasized Chobert's testimony, telling the jury they could "trust" Chobert because "he knows what he saw." The prosecutor sug-

gested that Chobert's testimony was given without anyone having influenced him, telling the jury: "Do you think that anybody
could get him to say anything that wasn't the truth? I would not
criticize that man one bit. . . . What motivation would Robert
Chobert have to make up a story. . . ." However, subsequent
revelations suggest that Chobert had substantial reasons to
ingratiate himself with the authorities by corroborating their
version of events.

Mark Scanlan

In one of his original statements to the police, Scanlan stated several times that he did not know whether Abu-Jamal or
his brother shot Faulkner: "I don't know who had the gun. I
don't know who fired it." He also misidentified Abu-Jamal as
the driver of the vehicle stopped by Officer Faulkner and was
approximately 120 feet from the scene. A diagram that Scanlan drew for police indicated that Abu-Jamal and Faulkner were
facing each other when the first shot was fired, contrary to the
prosecution's theory that the police officer was initially shot in
the back. At trial, Scanlan admitted that he had been drinking
on the night in question and that "There was confusion when all
three of them were in front of the car."

The missing witnesses

Abu-Jamal's attorneys also allege that a number of eyewitness were not investigated by the defense because of a lack
of resources and that the witnesses' whereabouts were withheld from them by the prosecution. According to subsequent
investigations by the current defense team, numerous witness-

es have been located who claim to have seen other unidentified men fleeing the scene of the killing. Since this report is primarily concerned with the fairness of Abu-Jamal's original trial, Amnesty International has not analyzed the statements of these potential witnesses. The defense filed an appellate brief in federal court in October 1999 which summarizes these claims.[32]

William Cook, Abu-Jamal's brother and an obvious eyewitness to the killing, did not testify for either side at trial. He was convicted in separate proceedings of assaulting Faulkner. Cook made a statement to the police on the night of the shooting, and another to Abu-Jamal's legal team in 1995. However, neither of these statements have been seen by Amnesty International. Abu-Jamal's supporters have alleged that in 1982, Cook was being intimidated by the police and feared being charged in connection with the killing and was therefore too frightened to testify. Cook was scheduled to testify during the 1995 hearing but failed to appear. Again it was alleged that this was due to fear of the police and of being arrested on unrelated charges in court. In his written denial of the 1995 appeal, Judge Sabo made negative assumptions regarding Cook's unwillingness to testify. Since 1995, the defense team have been unable to locate Cook despite numerous attempts.

The ballistics evidence

Although all five bullets in Abu-Jamal's gun were spent, the police failed to conduct tests to ascertain whether the weapon had been fired in the immediate past. The test is relatively simple: smell the gun for the odor of gunpowder, which should be detectable for approximately five hours after the gun was fired. Compounding this error, the police also failed to conduct chemical tests on Abu-Jamal's hands to find out if he had fired a gun recently.

The police appeared to be aware of the value of basic forensic testing. According to the testimony of Arnold Howard during the 1995 hearings, after he was arrested on suspicion of involvement in the Faulkner shooting, the police tested his hands to ascertain if he had fired a gun in the recent past. Howard was arrested because his driver's license application form was in Faulkner's possession.

As noted earlier, the court refused to grant the defense funding sufficient to obtain expert witnesses. As a consequence, the jury was presented with no expert testimony to counter the prosecution's assertion that Abu-Jamal had fired at Officer Faulkner and that the policeman was killed with Abu-Jamal's weapon.

The prosecution maintained that Officer Faulkner turned and fired at Abu-Jamal as he fell to the ground after being shot. Therefore, the entry of the bullet into Abu-Jamal should have been on a level or upward trajectory. However, according to the medical records, the overall pathway of the bullet was downwards. During trial, the doctor who removed the bullet from Abu-Jamal (who admitted his lack of forensic expertise) was asked why the bullet would be "unnecessarily lowered in its trajectory" and speculated that "ricochet" and "tumble" were the explanation.

In 1992, an expert forensic pathologist employed by Abu-Jamal's defense team examined the medical records and concluded:

. . . For these reasons, there appears to be no reasons to postulate a ricochet to explain a downward course through the body. Rather, it is likely that the bullet had a downward course through the body because of the relative positions of Mr. Jamal and the shooter. Consistent relative positions include a standing shooter firing down on a prone Mr. Jamal, or a standing shooter firing horizontally at Mr. Jamal while Mr. Jamal was bent over at the waist.

Neither of these postures is consistent with the prosecution's theory. The forensic pathologist also concluded that "since I disagree with both the Medical Examiner's findings with respect to the cause of death and Dr. Coletta's postulation of a possible 'ricochet' . . . Mr. Jamal's defense required, and would have been well served by, the testimony of a qualified forensic pathologist."

There were also inconsistencies in the original findings concerning the bullet removed from Faulkner's body. The Medical Examiner first wrote in his notes that the bullet was ".44 cal." (Abu-Jamal's gun was a .38 calibre weapon and could not possibly have fired such a bullet.) This discrepancy, which was never made known to the jury, was later explained by the Medical Examiner as "part of the paper work but not an official finding." At trial, the Medical Examiner testified that the bullet was consistent with those fired by Abu-Jamal's gun but that tests were inconclusive as to whether it actually came from his firearm. The court accepted the medical examiner as a ballistics expert. However, during the 1995 hearing, Judge Sabo contended that the medical examiner was "not a ballistics expert" and that his original findings that the bullet was a .44 caliber were a "mere lay guess."

In a case where the prosecution's theory of the crime rests on a specific sequence of events involving an exchange of gunfire, the gathering of ballistics evidence is crucial—as is the ability of the defense to present its own expert testimony on the significance of that evidence. The failure of the police to test Abu-Jamal's gun, hands and clothing for evidence of recent firing is deeply troubling. Without the ability to hear and assess that missing evidence, the jury was required to reach a verdict based largely on the contradictory and variable testimony of a limited list of eyewitnesses.

The sentence: condemned to death by free speech?
All persons are equal before the law. . . . In this respect, the law shall prohibit any discrimination and guarantee all persons equal and effective protection against discrimination on any grounds such as . . . political or other opinions. . . .[33]

Following a guilty verdict in a death penalty case, the majority of trial courts in the USA are required to convene a separate penalty phase hearing, during which the prosecution and defense present evidence and testimony arguing for and against a sentence of death. If the jury finds that the aggravating factors supporting execution outweigh the mitigating factors supporting leniency, they are required to impose a death sentence. Under Pennsylvania law, if even one juror disagrees with that finding a death sentence may not be imposed.

Like so much of Mumia Abu-Jamal's trial, the penalty phase was hurried and brief, lasting less than two hours. The jury then took less than three and a half hours to deliberate over Abu-Jamal's sentence.[34]

Although Abu-Jamal took the witness stand during the penalty phase, he limited his statements to objecting to various aspects of the trial that he believed were unfair and prejudicial to him, and to asserting his innocence. While his decision to testify as he did may thus have diminished his prospects for a life sentence, Jackson's defense of Abu-Jamal at this crucial phase of the trial was virtually nonexistent. He called no character witnesses, despite the availability of a State Representative for Philadelphia who would have testified concerning Abu-Jamal's "positive influence on the community" and "his advocacy respecting the need for the different ethnic and racial communities to work in harmony."[35] At no point did Jackson discuss a strategy for developing mitigating factors before the jury with Abu-Jamal's mother and sister, both of whom were prepared to testify on his behalf.

The secret monitoring of Mumia Abu-Jamal

During the penalty phase, the prosecution used Mumia Abu-Jamal's purported political beliefs and statements he made as a teenager against him. These statements were made 12 years before the trial and had no bearing on the case. The prosecution quoted from remarks attributed to Abu-Jamal in a newspaper article when he was a 16-year-old member of the Black Panther Party, which included the quotation from Mao Tse Tung that "political power grows out of the barrel of a gun." When questioning Abu-Jamal about his statements, the prosecutor suggested the remark "might ring a bell as to whether or not you are an executioner or endorse such actions."

During his summation of the case to the jury, the prosecutor cited Mumia Abu-Jamal's alleged political statements as a youth to argue for a death sentence, surmising that the defendant had held a long-standing desire to kill a police officer. The prosecutor clearly implied that Mumia Abu-Jamal's statements indicated his potential to kill a police officer:

> Anybody can grasp or hold any kind of philosophy you want. That's fine. That's what this country happens to be all made of. But, one thing that cannot be tolerated is constant abuse of authority and daily law breaking. That simply is not permitted.

Given that Mumia Abu-Jamal had no prior convictions for any offense, or any history of involvement in politically motivated violence, this reasoning was highly prejudicial and improper.

The US Supreme Court has determined that the prosecution's use of a defendant's political beliefs during the sentencing phase of a death penalty trial violates the US Constitution's First Amendment: the right to freedom of speech. In *Dawson v. Delaware* (1992), the Court ruled that the prosecution's introduction of Dawson's membership [in] a "white racist prison gang" (the Aryan Brotherhood) during the penalty phase was unconstitutional. "Whatever label is given to the evidence presented . . . Dawson's First Amendment rights were violated by the admission of the Aryan Brotherhood evidence . . . because

the evidence proved nothing more than Dawson's abstract beliefs," the Supreme Court ruled.

Amnesty International believes that any risk that the jury
may have been improperly influenced in favor of the death penalty is unacceptable and should constitute grounds for revers-
ing Abu-Jamal's death sentence.

The appeal to the Pennsylvania Supreme Court

Mumia Abu-Jamal first appealed his conviction and sentence to
the Pennsylvania Supreme Court in 1989, citing a number of er-
rors and irregularities in the trial proceedings. The appeal was
denied on all grounds.

The Court found no error in the prosecutor's references in
his summation to Mumia Abu-Jamal's past political affiliations
and statements. The Court denied the appeal, ruling that "Pun-
ishing a person for expressing his views or for associating with
certain people is substantially different from allowing . . . evidence of [the defendant's] character [to be considered] where
that character is a relevant inquiry." The Delaware Supreme
Court cited, and adopted verbatim, the Pennsylvania Supreme
Court's ruling in the Abu-Jamal case to deny the appeal of Delaware death row prisoner David Dawson. It would now appear
that the US Supreme Court has found fault with the Pennsylvania
Supreme Court's logic, through its ruling in *Dawson v. Delaware*.

The Pennsylvania Supreme Court also rejected Mumia
Abu-Jamal's claim that the prosecutor had acted improperly
when he had attempted to lessen the jury's responsibility for
imposing a death sentence by referring to the lengthy appeals
process, telling them:

Ladies and gentleman, you are not asked to kill anybody.
You are asked to follow the law. The same law that I keep
throwing at you, saying those words, law and order. I
should point out to you it's the same law that has for six
months provided safeguards for this defendant. The same
law that will provide him appeal after appeal after appeal .
. . [because of] the same law . . . nobody has died in Pennsylvania since 1962.

In a previous case also presided over by Judge Sabo (*Commonwealth v. Baker*), and involving the same prosecutor, Jo-
seph McGill, the prosecution also described the lengthy appeals
of death row inmates in his summation to the jury. In 1986
the Pennsylvania Supreme Court overturned Baker's death sentence, on the grounds that such language "minimiz[ed] the jury's sense of responsibility for a verdict of death."[36] The court
then reversed this precedent in 1989 by upholding Abu-Jamal's
death sentence, only to reestablish it in 1990, in the case of
Commonwealth v. Beasley, ordering the "precluding of all remarks about the appellate process in all future trials." This contradictory series of precedents leaves the disturbing impression
that the Court invented a new standard of procedure to apply it
to one case only: that of Mumia Abu-Jamal.

Abu-Jamal's appeal also argued that the withdrawal of the
court's permission for the defendant to represent himself violated his constitutional rights. In response, the Pennsylvania
Supreme Court stated: "The trial court noted at the time of *voir
dire* [jury selection] that several of the potential jurors were obviously shaken by Appellant's questioning. Appellant also re-

fused to adhere to proper procedure during this *voir dire*. . . ." This conclusion is not supported by the trial transcript.

The Court further held that Abu-Jamal did not have a guaranteed right to self-representation, since indigent defendants do not have the right to a lawyer of their own choosing:

> While an accused is constitutionally guaranteed the right to the assistance of counsel that right gives to a defendant only the right to choose, *at his or her own cost*, any attorney desired. Where, as here, an accused is indigent, the right involves counsel, but not free counsel of choice. (Emphasis in original.)

The Pennsylvania Supreme Court also denied Abu-Jamal's claim that the trial court's failure to require Officer Wakshul to testify amounted to a violation of a defendant's right to call exculpatory witnesses (i.e. witnesses that would help to prove his innocence). The Court based its decision on four grounds: Wakshul's claim that he had not reported the confession because he was in an emotional state over the death of Faulkner had been found credible by Judge Sabo and the state Supreme Court Justices had no reason to doubt that finding; Wakshul's account of the events was independent of Priscilla Durham's statement; Jackson's failure to call Wakshul at an earlier time, thereby ensuring his appearance in court, did not amount to "ineffective assistance of counsel" because it was Abu-Jamal's decision to call the witness at the last minute, and that Wakshul's testimony would have damaged Abu-Jamal by confirming the other two witnesses' account of the "confession."

By failing to compel Officer Wakshul to testify, the courts deprived the defense of the opportunity to cross-examine a key witness whose initial report of Abu-Jamal's behavior at the hospital is blatantly contradicted by his subsequent statements. Without hearing his sworn testimony, the jury was unable to properly assess the credibility of a central element of the prosecution's case: Abu-Jamal's alleged "confession." As discussed earlier, the jury's response to the alleged confession may have played a pivotal role in their deliberations during both phases of the trial.

In October 1998, the Pennsylvania Supreme Court denied Abu-Jamal's last appeal in state court. The case is now entering the federal court system for the final stages of appellate review. Concern has been raised over the strong links between members of the Pennsylvania Supreme Court and the local law enforcement community, as well as the previous involvement of one member of the Court in the prosecution of Mumia Abu-Jamal. These unresolved concerns and the Court's own rulings on Abu-Jamal's appeals have left the unfortunate impression that the state Supreme Court may have been unable to impartially adjudicate this controversial case.

Prior to the Court ruling on Abu-Jamal's appeal in 1998, his attorneys requested that Justice Ron Castille not participate in the deliberations. Justice Castille is a former Philadelphia District Attorney who opposed Abu-Jamal's earlier appeals; as the District Attorney, his name appeared on the appeal briefs which expressly advocated the position that Abu-Jamal's trial was fair and that the evidence against him was compelling. He was openly endorsed by the Fraternal Order of Police (FOP) for election to the Supreme Court. When refusing to recuse himself, Justice Castille made the following statement:

> I note that the very same FOP which endorsed me during earlier electoral processes also endorsed Mr. Chief Justice John P. Flaherty, Mr. Justice Ralph Cappy, Mr. Justice Russell M. Nigro, and Madame Justice Sandra Schultz Newman. If the FOP's endorsement constituted a basis for recusal, practically the entire court would be required to decline participation in this appeal.

The refusal of a judge to recuse himself from proceedings in which he previously served as an advocate for one of the parties is a serious breach of judicial ethics. Amnesty International deeply regrets Judge Castille's decision, particularly in light of the many concerns that have surfaced in the Mumia Abu-Jamal case over apparent judicial bias during the trial itself.

The Fraternal Order of Police: leading the call for the execution of Mumia Abu-Jamal

"If you don't like it you can join him [Abu-Jamal]. We'll take out the electric chair, we'll make it an electric couch. Our position on this will not brook any type of equivocation, any delay or anything else." —Richard Costello, President of the Philadelphia Fraternal Order of Police.[37]

The Philadelphia Fraternal Order of Police (FOP) has continually campaigned for Abu-Jamal's execution.[38] The organization has also reacted with hostility to the many prominent people calling for a new trial for Abu-Jamal. In August 1999, the FOP's national biennial general meeting passed a resolution calling for an economic boycott of all individuals and businesses that had expressed support for freeing Abu-Jamal. A spokesman for the organization stated: "It is wrong to allow companies and individuals to profit from the murder of an officer who made the ultimate sacrifice by trying to protect and serve the citizens of his community. And we will not rest until Abu-Jamal burns in hell." The FOP has strong ties with the state judiciary that adjudicated Abu-Jamal's appeals (see below). In 1994, Pennsylvania State Representative Mike McGeehan was quoted as stating: "I want to see Mumia Abu-Jamal die. I don't care how many Hollywood types are for him, we're going to see him die in Pennsylvania."[39]

The administration of capital justice in the USA is highly politicised and support for the death penalty is seen by many politicians and judicial officials as popular with the electorate; significantly, most state court judges and prosecutors must run for election in order to obtain or retain their positions.[40] Where the judiciary is part of the political process, the support or opposition of the law enforcement community for candidates can significantly affect both the outcome of judicial elections and the decisions of elected officials in death penalty cases.

In Pennsylvania, the justices who serve on the state Supreme Court are elected to their positions. Given the politicized nature of the death penalty in the USA, Amnesty International remains concerned about the political support received by members of the Pennsylvania Supreme Court by a law enforcement community so vigorously committed to the execution of Mumia Abu-Jamal.[41]

The law enforcement community's support for some members of the Court is both prominent and extensive: Chief Justice John P. Flaherty has been presented with a Justice Award by the Sheriffs' Association of Pennsylvania; Justice Ralph J. Cappy (who wrote the opinion denying Abu-Jamal a new trial) has been awarded "Man of the Year" by Pennsylvania State Police and "Man of the Year" by Pennsylvania Fraternal Order of Police; Justice Ronald D. Castille has been awarded a "Distinguished Public Service Award" by the Pennsylvania County and State Detectives Association, a "Layman Award" by the Pennsylvania Chiefs of Police Association and "Man of the Year" by Fraternal Order of Police Lodge No. 5 (Philadelphia); Justice Sandra Schultz Newman was honoured by the Police Chiefs Association of Southeastern Pennsylvania for "dedicated leadership and outstanding contributions to the community and law enforcement."

Were any of the Court's members to vote to uphold Abu-Jamal's appeals, these strong affiliations with a highly influential organization lobbying for Abu-Jamal's execution raises the probability that they would suffer a severe political backlash from the media and other politicians, thereby jeopardising their future on the bench.[42]

Mumia Abu-Jamal's appeals at the state level are now exhausted, and his case has entered the federal courts. Under the terms of the Anti-Terrorism and Effective Death Penalty Act (AEDPA), which President Clinton signed into law in 1996, the federal appellate courts must defer to the findings of the state courts of appeal in all but the most exceptional circumstances.[43] It remains unclear whether the restrictions of the AEDPA apply broadly to cases tried prior to its enactment. The federal courts that are preparing to review Mumia Abu-Jamal's appeals may thus be bound by the suspect rulings of the lower courts, even when deciding on crucial issues that received cursory or unsatisfactory review at the state level.

The record in this case indicates a pattern of events that compromised Abu-Jamal's right to a fair trial, including irregularities in the police investigation and the prosecution's presentation of the case, the possible coercion or exclusion of key witnesses, the appearance of judicial bias and the state's failure to provide the means necessary for an adequate defense. Years of appellate review have failed to allay or address these fundamental concerns, nor is it certain that the federal courts will be empowered to grant relief.

Under sentence of death: conditions on Pennsylvania's death row

The UN Economic and Social Council has urged states which retain the death penalty to "effectively apply the (UN) Standard Minimum Rules for the Treatment of Prisoners, in order to keep to a minimum the suffering of prisoners under sentence of death and to avoid any exacerbation of such suffering."[44]

In 1997, the Secretary General of Amnesty International, Pierre Sané, visited death rows in Texas and Pennsylvania. In both prisons he witnessed the appalling conditions and regimes inflicted on condemned inmates.[45]

In State Correctional Institution Greene (SCI Greene), the Secretary General met with death row inmates Mumia Abu-Jamal and Scott Blystone. At a press conference following the visit, Pierre Sané described SCI Greene: "Death row in Pennsylvania looks and feels like a morgue. Everything is high-tech, and there is no human being in sight. From the moment that condemned prisoners arrive, the state tries to kill them slowly, mechanically and deliberately—first spiritually, and then physically."

Scott Blystone described to the delegation the intense strain of undergoing preparation for execution, a process both he and Abu-Jamal suffered in 1995:

> They [the guards] come to your cell, you know you're getting a [death] warrant because they're real polite. They handcuff you, belt you and shackle your feet. It's silent, you can hear your heart beating. They take you to death watch—cells surrounded by plexiglass walls so sound can't get through. There's a camera at the front of your cell that watches you 24 hours a day. You're standing there alive and they're asking you where to send your body. After surviving a death warrant I felt like I'd lost my soul—it kills part of you.

Both Mumia Abu-Jamal and Scott Blystone told the delegation about widespread and frequent brutality inflicted upon prisoners by prison guards in SCI Greene, a long-term concern of Amnesty International. In May 1998 four SCI Greene guards were fired from their jobs and at least a further 21 were demoted, suspended or reprimanded because of their treatment of inmates.

SCI Greene is in a predominantly white rural area; 93 per

cent of prison staff are white. However, the vast majority of the inmates are African Americans or Hispanics from urban areas, leading to high levels of racial tension and allegations of racial abuse. A newspaper article written following the sacking of the guards, quoting from both guards and prisoners, detailed regular occurrences of racism and violence by prison workers.[46] The allegations included guards beating prisoners and then writing KKK (i.e. Ku Klux Klan) with the inmate's blood; the "working over" (beating) of certain prisoners by guards upon the instruction of superior officers to "adjust their attitudes;" and guards spitting tobacco juice into inmates' food.

Despite assurances received from the Pennsylvania Department of Corrections (in a reply to a letter concerning the abuse of women prisoners on death row in SCI Muncy) that prison guards act in a professional manner towards condemned inmates, Amnesty International continues to receive complaints from prisoners. For example, in September 1999, the organization received detailed allegations of racist abuse directed at condemned prisoners in SCI Greene, including accounts of prisoners refusing to eat food served by the guards on a specific shift who were placing "nonfood" items in meals.

On October 13, 1999, Governor Ridge of Pennsylvania signed a death warrant ordering Abu-Jamal's execution on December 2, 1999. Amnesty International believes the execution order was signed solely for political reasons as the governor would have been aware that Abu-Jamal was to file an appeal within the next two weeks that would automatically stayed the execution. In a statement, Amnesty International drew a comparison between the governor's act and the act of torture: "This death warrant serves no purpose except to put Mumia Abu-Jamal on 'death watch'—causing him unnecessary suffering. This is playing politics with a man's life. The unnecessary infliction of suffering upon a prisoner by a government official constitutes torture."

SCI Greene prison authorities: violating Abu-Jamal's right to secure communications with his legal team.

All US prisoners have the right to exchange information with their legal representatives in confidentiality. In 1995, prison authorities admitted they had copied privileged mail sent by attorneys to Abu-Jamal, on the grounds that they were investigating a rule violation by him. In 1996, a district court ruled that such acts "actually injured" Abu-Jamal and were in violation of his Constitutional rights under the Sixth and Fourteenth Amendments.

This right is also protected under Principle 8 of the UN's Basic Principles on the Roles of Lawyers.

Conclusion

"Capital punishment may only be carried out pursuant to a final judgment rendered by a competent court after a legal process which gives all possible safeguards to ensure a fair trial, at least equal to those contained in article 14 of the International Covenant on Civil and Political Rights. . . ."[47]

For the diminishing list of countries which still resort to the death penalty, international human rights standards require the very highest level of fairness in capital cases, given the irreversible nature of the penalty.

The trial of Mumia Abu-Jamal took place in an atmosphere of animosity and tension, much of it directed against the defendant. As the judge at the first pretrial hearing stated: "I know there are certain cases that have explosive tendencies in this community, and this is one of them." That animosity has endured throughout the 17 years since the trial, particularly within the law enforcement community. In 1995, upon learning of Mumia Abu-Jamal's stay of execution, Philadelphia police officer James Green said: "It makes you wonder. Maybe we should have executed him at 13th and Locust [the crime scene] where he executed Danny Faulkner."[48]

The law enforcement community's unseemly agitation for the execution of Mumia Abu-Jamal is just one of Amnesty International's concerns over this case.

Many of the deficiencies that Amnesty International has identified in the Mumia Abu-Jamal case mirror broader concerns over the application of the death penalty nationwide. Concern about possible judicial bias is not limited to Pennsylvania, and the resources provided to indigent defendants are pitifully inadequate in many jurisdictions. Police misconduct has been cited in many cases, and the risk of wrongful convictions in capital trials remains alarmingly high.

Amnesty International remains concerned that the relationship between the Pennsylvania judiciary and the law enforcement community at the very least gives rise to the unfortunate impression that justice is a one-way street leading to Mumia Abu-Jamal's eventual execution. The Pennsylvania Supreme Court, for example, appears to have ignored its own previous precedents in denying the defendant's appeals.

Proponents of the execution of Abu-Jamal maintain that he had a "fair" trial and was duly convicted and sentenced by a jury of his peers. The adversarial system of justice in the USA can only be a fair arbiter if the defense and prosecution have reasonable access to the resources necessary to present their version of events, and if the judge overseeing the case is truly neutral. Juries can only be accurate assessors of events if they are given a complete view of the facts—including any differing explanations and interpretations of events—and are made aware of the possible reasons for the bias of witnesses. These factors were clearly missing in Abu-Jamal's trial.

During the trial of Mumia Abu-Jamal, the jury was left unaware of much of the crucial information regarding the death of Officer Faulkner.

Other factors present during the prosecution of this case also render the verdict and sentence fundamentally unsound, including inadequate trial representation, the overt hostility of the trial judge and the appearance of judicial bias during appellate review.

Based on its review of the trial transcript and other original documents, Amnesty International has determined that numerous aspects of this case clearly failed to meet minimum international standards safeguarding the fairness of legal proceedings. Amnesty International therefore believes that the interests of justice would best be served by the granting of a new trial to Mumia Abu-Jamal. The trial should fully comply with international standards of justice and should not allow for the re-imposition of the death penalty. The organization is also recommending that the retrial take place in a neutral venue, where the case has not polarized the public as it has in Philadelphia. Finally, the authorities should permit prominent jurists from outside the USA to observe the proceedings, to ensure that the retrial complies in all respects with universally-recognized human rights safeguards.

Endnotes

1. For further information see "Rights for All," AI index AMR 51/35/98, ISBN 0 86210 274 X, published October 1998.
2. For example, in 1995, six Philadelphia police officers pleaded guilty to charges of planting illegal drugs on suspects, the theft of more than $100,000, and the falsification of reports. The investigations into the officers' actions have led to the release of hundreds of defendants whose convictions were overturned by the appeal courts. Also in 1995, two other officers from Philadelphia received prison sentences of five to 10 years for framing young men. Since 1993, the city of Philadelphia has paid out approximately $27 million in more than 230 lawsuits alleging police misconduct.
3. *Above the Law: Police and Excessive Use of Force*, Jerome H. Skolnick and James J. Fyfe, published by The Free Press.
4. *Frank Rizzo: The Last Big Man in Big City America*, S.A. Paolantonio, pubished by Camino Books.
5. The MOVE organization formed in Philadelphia during the early 1970s. The group follows the teaching of John Africa. Its manifesto includes: "MOVE work is to stop industry from poisoning the air . . . and to put an end to the enslavement of life . . . the purpose of John Africa's revolution is to show people how corrupt, rotten, criminally enslaving this system is . . . and to set the example of revolution for people to follow when they realize how they've been oppressed, repressed, duped, tricked by this system, this government and see the need to rid themselves of this cancerous system as MOVE does." (Description taken from *25 Years on the MOVE*, published by MOVE.)
6. A similar incident occurred in 1985, when a standoff developed between police and members of MOVE. The siege was ended when a police helicopter dropped an incendiary device on the house, killing 11 of its occupants, including six children (only two occupants survived). The device also started a fire that destroyed over 60 houses in the predominantly black area. In 1995, a federal jury awarded MOVE members $1.5 million after determining that the city of Philadelphia had violated their constitutional right to protection against unreasonable search and seizure when the police dropped the bomb.
7. Amnesty International has long-term concerns around COINTEL-PRO. In 1981, the organization called for a commission of inquiry

into FBI operations which it believed had undermined the fairness of trials involving several BPP members and members of the American Indian Movement. Amnesty International also called for a retrial for Geronimo Ji-Jaga Pratt when evidence came to light after his trial that he had been targeted for "neutralization" by COINTELPRO. Pratt was released from prison in 1998 after 27 years in prison when his conviction was overturned on appeal because of new evidence showing that the key prosecution's witness was a police informer (which he had denied while testifying).

In 1995, defense lawyers obtained approximately 700 pages of files on Mumia Abu-Jamal maintained by the Federal Bureau of Investigation (FBI), via the Freedom of Information Act. These documents represented only a portion of the total files and were heavily censored.

The FBI began monitoring Abu-Jamal in 1969 when he was 15 years old, because of his activities at high school and later with the Black Panther Party (BPP). According to a sworn affidavit by the attorney who examined the files, Abu-Jamal was under surveillance as part of the FBI's Counterintelligence Program, COINTELPRO, which operated with the cooperation and assistance of the Philadelphia police. According to the affidavit: "Mr. Jamal was subjected to surveillance, harassment, disruption, politically motivated arrests and attempted frame-ups by the FBI, who worked in conjunction with the Philadelphia Police Department." Although the FBI classified Abu-Jamal as "armed and dangerous", he was not convicted of any crime during this period. The documents reveal that the FBI was continuing to monitor Abu-Jamal as late as 1990, recording the details of one of his visitors while he was incarcerated [at] Huntingdon Prison.

8. *Philadelphia Inquirer*, December 10, 1981.

9. Principle 2 of the Basic Principles on the Independence of the Judiciary. Adopted by the Seventh United Nations Congress on the Prevention of Crime and the Treatment of Offenders, held in Milan from August 26 to September 6, 1985 and endorsed by General Assembly resolutions 40/32 of 29 November 1985, and resolutions 40/146 of December 13, 1985.

10. See "The secret monitoring of Mumia Abu-Jamal" for more information regarding the Fraternal Order of Police.

11. Of the 124 prisoners from Philadelphia on death row in October 1998, only 15 were white. Studies of the administration of the

death penalty in the USA have consistently found evidence that race of defendant and/or victim can play a major role in who is sentenced to die. One such study found that, even after making allowances for case differences, blacks in Philadelphia were substantially more likely to receive death sentences than other defendants who committed similar murders (D. Baldus, et al., "Race Discrimination and the Death Penalty in the Post Furman Era: An Empirical and Legal Overview, with Preliminary Findings from Philadelphia," *Cornell Law Review*, Volume 83, September 1998).

12. *What price justice?: Poor defendants pay the cost as courts save money on murder trials*, published September 13, 1992.

13. "Guilty and Framed," Stuart Taylor Jr., *The American Lawyer*, published December 1995.

14. Principle 13 of the Basic Principles on the Role of Lawyers, adopted by consensus at the Eighth United Nations Congress on the Prevention of Crime and the Treatment of Offenders in 1990 and welcomed by the UN General Assembly.

15. For example, George McFarland was tried and sentenced to death in Texas in 1991. At trial he was represented by a lawyer who continually fell asleep during the proceedings. When asked about the lawyer sleeping, the trial judge explained that this did not violate McFarland's constitutional right   to be represented because "the Constitution does not say the lawyer has to be awake." For further information see "Is Fairness Irrelevant? The Evisceration of Federal Habeas Corpus Review and Limits on the Ability of State Courts to Protect Fundamental Rights," Stephen B. Bright, *Washington and Lee Law Review*, Vol. 54, No. 1 (Winter 1997).

16. International Commission of Jurists, "Administration of the death penalty in the United States. Report of a Mission," June 1996. For more information see "USA: A macabre assembly line of death: Death penalty developments in 1997," AI index AMR 51/20/98, published April 1998.

17. Comments of the HRC: USA, UN Doc. CCPR/C/79/Add.50, April 7, 1995, para. 23. The ICCPR was signed by the USA on October 5, 1977, and ratified on June 8, 1992. In 1997, the UN Special Rapporteur on extrajudicial, summary and arbitrary executions also stated that the "lack of adequate counsel and legal representation for many capital defendants is disturbing," following his visit to the USA in 1997. UN Doc E/CN.4/1998/68/Add.3

18. Despite the subsequent introduction of competency standards

for appointed counsel, the administration of the death penalty in Pennsylvania continues to be a major concern to Amnesty International and other organizations. In 1997, the Philadelphia Bar Association passed a resolution calling for a general moratorium on the use of the death penalty. The resolution cited the "substantial risk that the death penalty continues to be imposed in an arbitrary, capricious and discriminatory manner" and called upon the moratorium to continue until "such time as the fair and impartial administration of the death penalty can be ensured and the risk that innocent persons may be executed is minimized."

19. Article 14(3)(d) of the International Covenant on Civil and Political Rights, ratified by the USA in 1992, states: "In the determination of any criminal charges against him, everyone shall be entitled to the following minimum guarantees, in full equality: . . . (d)To be tried in his presence, and to defend himself in person or through legal assistance of his own choosing. . . .

20. John Africa had successfully represented himself against federal charges of illegal ownership of weapons in 1981.

21. Judge Sabo also sanctioned lawyers representing Abu-Jamal in the 1995 hearing, fining one and temporarily imprisoning another. It is extremely rare for judges to sanction lawyers in the USA.

22. Article 8(2)(f) of the American Convention on Human Rights. The USA signed the Convention but has yet to ratify it.

23. Numerous other states, such as California, provide two attorneys in death penalty cases. The American Bar Association's "Guidelines for the Appointment and Performance of Counsel in Death Penalty Cases" specifies "In cases where the death penalty is sought, two qualified attorneys should be assigned to represent the defendant."

24. Pretrial hearing on April 1, 1982. A calendar judge sets the schedule for the trial and oversees the granting of funds to the defense attorneys for experts, etc.

25. Amnesty International has recorded many instances of the pitifully inadequate resources afforded by the state to capital defendants across the USA. The funding provided by the city of Philadelphia for legitimate defense expenses in capital cases is particularly deficient. In 1992, the Death Penalty Information Center (DPIC) published *Justice on the Cheap: The Philadelphia Story*. The report detailed many examples of inadequate defense funding in capital trials in Philadelphia, concluding that "any pretense to equal justice

is fatally undermined" and that "justice is becoming ever more just another commodity available only to the few who can afford it." The report is available from DPIC, 1320 Eighteenth Street, NW Washington, DC, USA, or via the website www.essential.org/dpic

26. Alternate jurors are to be used in the event that a member of the jury is unable to take part in the deliberations because of illness, misconduct, etc.

27. *Batson v. Kentucky*. For further information see "Killing with Prejudice: Race and the Death Penalty in the USA," p. 12, AI index AMR 51/52/99, published May 1999.

28. The jury was "sequestered" during the trial (housed in a hotel and forbidden contact with the outside world). The removal of jurors by the prosecution on the grounds of their race remains a common practice. Prosecutors simply give a vaguely plausible non-racial reason for dismissing the juror. One year after the *Batson* ruling, the Assistant District Attorney for Philadelphia made a training videotape for the city's prosecutors. On the video, he describes how to select a jury more likely to convict, including the removal of potential black jurors: "Let's face it, the blacks from the low-income areas are less likely to convict. There's a resentment to law enforcement. . . . You don't want those guys on your jury. . . . If you get a white teacher in a black school who's sick of these guys, that may be the one to accept." The video also instructed the trainee prosecutors on how to hide the racial motivation for the rejection of prospective jurors in order to avoid successful claims of racial discrimination from defense lawyers. The tape did not become public until 1997. A recent study of Philadelphia found that the likelihood of receiving a death sentence is nearly four times higher if the defendant is black. See "Killing with Prejudice" (footnote 27) for more details.

29. Dissenting in the case of Mexican national Cesar Fierro.

30. Officer Bell was Daniel Faulkner's police partner and "best friend." Priscilla Durham, who at first denied knowing Faulkner, later admitted that she had spoken to him on several occasions, sometimes over coffee.

31. Abu-Jamal's allegation that he was severely beaten by police has not been upheld. However, several police officers admitted during their trial testimony that they "accidentally" hit Abu-Jamal's head against a pole and dropped him on his face while carrying him to the police wagon.

32. The appeal brief can be found at http://mojo.calyx.net/~re-fuse/mumia/101699petition.html

33. Article 26 of the ICCPR.

34. The trial transcript for the sentencing hearing can be found at http://mojo.calyx.net/~refuse/mumia/082599july3trans.html

35. Sworn affidavit of former State Representative David P. Richardson, dated May 1995.

36. The Supreme Court also ruled that "the Commonwealth can only present evidence as to the aggravating circumstances set out in the [death penalty] statue" in the case of *Commonwealth v. Holcombin* 1985. The aggravating circumstances in the statue do not include a defendant's political views or comments.

37. Transcript of Channel 10 (WCAU) interview, July 14, 1990.

38. The Fraternal Order of Police is the nation's largest organization of law enforcement professionals, with more than 283,000 members.

39. Quoted in the *Philadelphia Daily News*, June 2, 1994.

40. Also see "Judges and the Politics of Death: Deciding Between the Bill of Rights and the Next Election in Capital Cases," by Stephen B. Bright and Patrick J. Keenan (*Boston University Law Review*, Volume 75, Number 3, May 1995). Also available at http://www.schr.org/reports/index.html

41. "The [UN Human Rights] Committee is concerned about the impact which the current system of election of judges may, in a few States, have on the implementation of the rights provided under article 14 of the [International] Covenant [on Civil and Political Rights] and welcomes the efforts of a number of States in the adoption of a selection system based on merit. . . ." "The Committee recommends that the current system in a few States of appointment of judges through elections be reconsidered with a view to its replacement by a system of appointment on merit by an independent body." Comments of the Human Rights Committee. CCPR/C/79/Add.50. Paragraphs 23 and 36.

42. Amnesty International has documented numerous occasions where judges were criticized, and sometimes removed from office by the electorate, for upholding the appeal of a condemned inmate. For example, Penny White was removed by the electorate from her position on the Tennessee Supreme Court after being attacked for her ruling overturning the death sentence of Richard Odom. For further information see "USA: Death penalty developments in

1996," AI index AMR 51/01/97. In October 1999, the US Senate rejected President Clinton's nomination of Ronnie White for the position of federal district judge. The Republican Senators all voted against White, citing what they perceived as his reluctance to vote to uphold death sentences. One Senator said: "During his tenure [on the Missouri Supreme Court], he has far more frequently dissented in capital cases than any other judge." (*Los Angeles Times*, October 5, 1999).

43. For more details on the Act please see "USA: Death penalty developments in 1996," AI index AMR 51/01/97, published March 1997.

44. ECOSOC Resolution 1996/15, adopted on July 23, 1996.

45. For details for the Secretary General's visit to Texas death row, please see "Lethal Injustice: the Death Penalty in Texas," AI index AMR 51/10/98, published March 1998.

46. "Firings and charges have shaken up SCI Greene," *Pittsburgh Post-Gazette*, August 11, 1998.

47. Paragraph 5, Safeguards guaranteeing protection of the rights of those facing the death penalty, adopted by the UN Economic and Social Council in resolution 1984/50 on May 25, 1984, and endorsed by the UN General Assembly in resolution 39/118, adopted without a vote on December 14, 1984.

48. Quoted in the *New York Times* on August 8, 1995. Amnesty International is appalled that a police officer would openly espouse the possibility of an extrajudicial execution.

ABOUT THE AUTHOR

Mumia Abu-Jamal is an award-winning journalist, political activist, and author. In 1981, he was elected president of the Association of Black Journalists (Philadelphia chapter) and was a radio reporter for National Public Radio (NPR). As part of a team of reporters at WHYY, one of NPR's premier stations, he won the prestigious Major Armstrong Award from Columbia University for excellence in broadcasting.

On December 9, 1981, Abu-Jamal was shot, arrested, and charged for killing a white police officer in Philadelphia. In 1982 he was convicted and sentenced to death in a trial that Amnesty International determined "clearly failed to meet minimum international standards safeguarding the fairness of legal proceedings." After he had spent over 28 years on death row, in 2011 Abu-Jamal's death sentence was vacated when the Supreme Court affirmed the decisions of four federal judges who had declared his death sentence unconstitutional. He is now serving a life sentence without the possibility of parole. Throughout his decades of imprisonment, most of which was spent in solitary confinement on death row, Abu-Jamal has steadfastly maintained his innocence.

Abu-Jamal obtained his GED in prison in July 1992; he earned his BA from Goddard College in January 1996; he was awarded an honorary Doctorate of Law degree from the New College of California in May 1996; and in 1999, he earned a Masters of Arts degree from California State University, Dominguez Hills. He is currently working on his Ph.D.

Abu-Jamal has produced radio commentaries with Prison Radio for decades, and has authored more than 10 books, including *Live From Death Row*, *We Want Freedom*, *Jailhouse Lawyers*, *The Classroom and the Cell*, *Murder Incorporated*, *Writing on the Wall*, and *Have Black Lives Ever Mattered?*

In late 2018, Abu-Jamal's right to appeal was reinstated by a Philadelphia judge. The ongoing fight for his freedom continues.

www.bringmumiahome.com
www.prisonradio.org/mumia-info